MARY BERRY'S
FREEZER
COOKBOOK

Other books by Mary Berry, published
by Piatkus

Mary Berry's Food Processor Cookbook
Mary Berry's Cookery Course
Mary Berry's Favourite Recipes
Mary Berry's Buffets

MARY BERRY'S
FREEZER
COOKBOOK

PIATKUS

My thanks go to Debbie Woolhead for her invaluable help in the preparation of this book, the first major collection of recipes we have worked on together. Debbie has become an expert on defrosting freezers and can complete the job in under an hour—essential considering the pressure they have been under during the last months.

Cover photograph shows Cheese Mouthfuls (page 57), Simple Lemon Syllabub (page 137), Garlic Herb Loaf (page 44), individual Cheese and Spinach Quiches (page 120) and Pissaladière (page 119).

Copyright © 1994 Mary Berry

First published in 1984 by
Judy Piatkus (Publishers) Ltd, 5 Windmill St,
London W1

This revised paperback edition first published in 1994
Reprinted 1996

**The moral right of the author
has been asserted**

*A Catalogue record for this
book is available from the
British Library*

ISBN 0 7499 1294 4

Set by The Professional Data Bureau, London SW17
Printed & bound in Great Britain by
The Bath Press Ltd, Bath, Avon

CONTENTS

List of illustrations

The publishers would like to thank the
following organisations for supplying photographs
for use in this book:

British Meat (facing p. 97)
The Milk Marketing Board (facing pp. 64 and 129)
Sea Fish Authority (facing p. 65)

Photographs facing pages 96 and 128 by Tim Imrie.

Making the most of your freezer

A freezer is part of my way of life and an absolutely essential piece of kitchen equipment for me now, and food freezing is something I do daily. Whether I'm testing recipes for television or feeding my family, I just don't know how I would manage without my freezer.

So in this book—which is not intended to be an encyclopedic work on freezing—I have gathered together many favourite recipes, old and new, which can be prepared for *now* and eaten with enjoyment; which can be doubled up, with some to be eaten now and some frozen for later; and many which can be prepared at leisure or on a baking/cooking day, and stored in the freezer for later.

I've been creating recipes for the freezer since the very beginning of my career, thus my own freezer is just like an extension of my storecupboard. To use it in this way is much more relaxing than using it as a bank where foods are sometimes forgotten. Money may accrue interest the longer it is on deposit, but food in a freezer just gathers ice crystals and loses quality after too long; make a rough note of what your family eats in a month, then you *know* what to freeze—that elaborate casserole in a wine sauce may be a bad investment if your family will not eat it!

And, to continue the store-cupboard simile, your freezer can also have ready, for almost instant use, many items which might not store well in other ways or which are fiddly or time-consuming to prepare—stock, grated cheese, croûtons, breadcrumbs and nuts, for instance.

Remember that your freezer is *your* slave, not the other way round. Use it and fill it (for it should be full, to run most economically) according to your own and your family's needs.

Packaging for the freezer

The purpose of packaging for the freezer is to exclude air and protect the food. Freezer burn, caused by exposure to air, causes dehydration of the food, discoloured patches, and a slowing down of the freezing process.

Polythene bags
Heavy-gauge polythene bags are thick enough to withstand low temperatures without splitting. They are not expensive, and are available in various sizes. Always exclude the air carefully before sealing the bag.

They can also be used for economy of space. Rectangular shapes take up least space in the freezer, so line a suitable container or box with a polythene bag, pour in the food, and freeze. Once frozen, the food can stack efficiently in the bag, and the container can be released for further kitchen duty!

Boil-in-bags

These can be bought from freezer centres for casseroles and sauces. They can be plunged straight from the freezer into boiling water. The prepared dish can be frozen in the sealed bag and then reheated with the minimum of fuss. Put two items in the same pan of water if you like, such as a chicken casserole and new potatoes in butter.

Twist ties

These are usually supplied with polythene bags. They are the simplest and most effective way of sealing food for the freezer.

Foil cases

Foil containers come in a variety of shapes and sizes. Some have their own lids, but others must be covered with foil. They are especially useful for complete meals, flans and pies which can be reheated in the container. Use them with caution for acidic foods, and *don't* take them from freezer to microwave. When putting the lid on remember to place white cardboard side uppermost as you can then write on the lid the freezing and thawing details with a waterproof pen.

Rigid containers

Rigid polythene containers are the best to use, but can be quite costly— although they last for (almost) ever. They protect food, and also stack easily in the freezer on top of each other. Icecream containers are not everlasting, but are a very good shape for storing foods. Save old margarine tubs, yoghurt pots, etc., for freezing smaller quantities of food. Food must be cool before being packed in any plastic containers as they do not withstand hot temperatures.

Foil and cling film

These are best for wrapping unusual shapes, such as joints of meat, as they mould around the food. Once wrapped it is best to put the food in a polythene bag too, and then seal with a twist tie. Cling film is particularly useful for interleaving between hamburgers and pancakes, say, and foil can be used to line a casserole dish before cooking, so that after cooking and freezing, the contents in the foil can be removed from the dish and carefully overwrapped for freezer storage.

Labelling

Over the years I have found it far better actually to write on the bag or container with a waterproof marker pen than on a label which is liable to fall off. There is *nothing* worse than a mysterious frozen parcel which completely lacks identity! Jot down the date, type of food, the number of people it will serve. If it is a particularly good casserole, then say so as you label it. Make a note of whether anything has to be added—soured cream, for instance, or snipped chives—when it is served, and include cooking instructions as well. The label should be as informative as possible, and then there will be no confusion when the dish comes out of the freezer.

Preparing food for the freezer

Be sure to let all food cool thoroughly first. Pack in appropriate quantities and containers. Some dishes such as casseroles or mince can be frozen in a shallow ovenproof dish then when firm removed from the dish (dip the base quickly into hot water if necessary to loosen the contents); wrap with foil, put into a polythene bag, seal and label then return to the freezer. Remove as much air as possible from the package before sealing. So that the freezing process is quick and even, use shallow containers in preference to deep ones.

Open freezing

This is a method of freezing certain types of food before it is packed, especially good for fish cakes, burgers, rissoles, vegetables etc. which could, annoyingly, freeze firmly together if packed in other ways. It's also very good for fruit which might otherwise freeze together—like strawberries or raspberries if packed when slightly wet.

Cakes should be open frozen so that the icing doesn't squash when being wrapped.

Open freezing makes storage easier ultimately. Open-frozen peas, for example, can be packed in one big bag, and then will flow freely from the bag when required. To open freeze, spread the food out on a baking tray then pack only when frozen solid.

The fast-freeze switch

This overrides the thermostat. I only use it when freezing more than 3lb (1.4kg) food or when I want to freeze some icecream quickly. Remember to switch it off again once the food is frozen.

Organising the freezer

Put the heaviest and least used foods, such as the turkey ready for Christmas, at the bottom of a chest freezer or at the back of an upright freezer. This saves having to lift them in and out each time you want something from the freezer.

Ideally have drawers or baskets to keep the different types of food in. As far as possible group foods into categories and pack them separately. Coloured polythene sacks are particularly good for separating foods: pack meat in a red sack, fish in a blue sack, vegetables in a green sack, etc. (Sacks and other polythene packaging are available from Lakeland Plastics, Windermere.)

Ideally in a chest freezer have special stacking baskets or improvise by making your own from old grocery boxes, and tie on string handles. Choose them all the same height so that they come to the same level in the freezer when stacked.

Keep one section of the freezer for storing all foods which need using in the near future, such as the odd piece of cake or ½ pint (300 ml) sauce.

Keeping a record

I used to advise using a little book for keeping a record of what there was in the freezer, but I now find it best to have a big board near the freezer. Mark down the food as you put it in the freezer then strike it off as you take it out. This way you always know what you have in stock. (But of course this presupposes that you have *room* for a big board ...!)

In case of emergency

Sellotape the name and telephone number of your local engineer or freezer centre on to your freezer in case it ever goes wrong. Although it is unlikely that you will ever need it, it is best to have it at hand. Before phoning first check that the plug hasn't been pulled out by mistake, or that there hasn't been a local power cut.

Defrosting the freezer

Defrost when there is ¼ inch (6mm) layer of frost near the lid or door, and *do* defrost then as putting it off for another time will always make the job seem far worse than it actually is. Defrosting also gives you an opportunity to sort everything out.

Plan of campaign

1. Switch off the freezer.

2. Bring your largest preserving pan of hot water to the boil.

3. Empty the freezer. Make a neat pile of the baskets, putting the icecream right in the middle as that will be the first to melt. Cover the whole lot with old rugs or sleeping bags. Insulate as thoroughly as you can.

4. Leave door or lid of freezer open. Put wad of newspaper on floor of freezer then put in a pan of hot water. The paper prevents the freezer from being damaged by the hot pan and will soak up the water as the frost melts. Close the lid or door.

5. Do another job in the house for 40 minutes. It may be necessary to put in another pan of hot water if the frost was very thick.

6. Sort out food into correct drawers and baskets.

7. Open lid or door of freezer. Remove pan. Mop up water and wipe out with mild detergent. Wipe dry with old towels. Close lid or door. Switch on and leave for 15 minutes.

8. Replace food and promise to keep it tidy!

Thawing food

I used to say thaw everything in the refrigerator—certainly some foods such as pâtés, mousses and casseroles, are best thawed in this way provided there is time. But a casserole in a polythene bag can take up to 2 days to defrost if the refrigerator is on a particularly cool setting. I now find the most practical place for thawing is in the larder or cupboard away from pets.

Although it is possible to reheat many foods from frozen, it is a waste of fuel and with something like a casserole it can easily stick and the meat can lose its texture. Generally, you should allow foods to thaw at room temperature.

Thawing times at room temperature

A casserole takes 6-8 hours

A cake takes 4-6 hours

A turkey takes 3 hours per pound (450g)

There are not many cases where food can be over-thawed, except with some fruits. Soft fruits—strawberries and raspberries, for instance—are best served well chilled whilst they are still firm.

The microwave and the freezer

First read your own manufacturer's instructions on using the microwave and freezer.

Thawing

With a microwave, thawing will take a fraction of the time usually required. It is therefore helpful to have a microwave when unexpected guests arrive or when you have forgotten to take the joint out of the freezer for dinner! When defrosting, the food defrosts from the outside as this is the part with which the microwaves first come in contact. To ensure even defrosting occasionally turn or stir the food; a microwave with a turn-table does this for you. The best microwaves have variable power so that the outside doesn't begin to cook before the inside has thawed. Alternate bursts of microwave energy with rest periods give the microwaves time to penetrate the food.

Thawing and cooking

Some foods may be cooked straight from frozen in the microwave—these include most vegetables—and this method is marvellous for small quantities. Fish can be cooked when partially thawed, but meat and poultry must be completely thawed before beginning to cook.

Defrosting times vary according to the shape of the frozen food or package, the weight and density of the food and the starting temperature.

Tips

1. Don't use metal or foil containers in the microwave. China, glass or plastic are the best to use.

2. Cover food with cling film or a glass cover to retain moisture.

3. Stir or turn round to ensure even defrosting.

4. Fish defrosts very quickly so only give short bursts of microwave energy.

Freezer know-how

Ten basic rules

1. Freeze only the best, good-quality foods at peak conditions. Food will come out in the same condition as it goes in. Freezing can't improve tatty food.

2. Cool food after cooking or blanching before freezing.

3. Exclude as much air as possible from the packaged food to prevent it drying out.

4. Pack and seal foods thoroughly otherwise the food will deteriorate in the freezer.

5. Freeze food quickly, packed in quantities that you are likely to need.

6. Label food properly with date, number of portions and what it is.

7. Once food is frozen, transfer to the section of the freezer that contains the same sort of food, i.e. keep all vegetables, meat and so on together. Keep a good rotation of stock in the freezer. Jot down as you put things in the freezer then just tick them off as you take them out.

8. Fast-freeze foods if you are freezing more than 3 lb (1.4 kg) of food at any one time. The fast-freeze switch overrides the thermostat and keeps the temperature low.

9. Once food has frozen solid return fast freeze to off to allow freezer to return to normal freezer storage temperature of 0°F (- 18°C)

10. Be ready for emergencies. Put the name of your maintenance engineer or service agent on a label or card stuck to the side of the freezer or other prominent place nearby. If the freezer isn't working, first check the plug; often it isn't pushed in properly, or there might be a localised power cut.

Storage times

Vegetables:

Most vegetables	12 months
Raw mushrooms	1 month
Cooked mushrooms	3 months
Onions	3-6 months

Fruit:

Most fruit	12 months
Unstoned fruit	3 months
Fruit pies	6 months

Uncooked meats:

Beef	8 months
large joints	10 months
Lamb	6 months
large joints	10 months
Pork	3 months
large joints	6 months
Mince	3 months
Bacon, vacuum packed	5 months
Sausages	2 months

Poultry:

Chicken	12 months
Duck	6 months
Game	12 months

Fish:

White fish	3 months
Oily fish	2 months

Cooked dishes:

Pies and casseroles 3 months (some keep in the freezer for less than 3 months, see recipe)

Puddings and desserts:

Most, on average	2 months
Icecream	2 months

Baked goods:

Cakes	3 months
Bread	3 months
Pastry	3 months
Sandwiches	2 months
Scones	2 months
Croûtons	6 months
Breadcrumbs	6 months

Dairy produce:

Frozen cream	3 months
Unsalted butter	6 months
Hard cheese	3 months
Rich cream cheese	6 weeks
Camembert	3 months
Brie	3 months

Liquids:

Soups	2 months
Sauces	2 months
Stocks	6 months

Freezing vegetables

Most vegetables freeze well for a year, or until the season comes round again. Only salad vegetables are not suitable for freezing. For best results only freeze vegetables which are young and freshly picked and of the finest quality.

Blanching and cooling facts

All vegetables freeze better if blanched. Blanching, or scalding, is a quick immersion in boiling water to preserve colour and flavour. It slows down enzyme action which can cause deterioration during storage, and is *not*, as some people assume, to destroy bugs and tenderise vegetables!

A blanching basket is ideal but not a necessity; a colander or a nylon muslin straining bag from a home-brewing shop can also be used.

A small quantity, not more than 1lb (450g) vegetables should be blanched at a time in 6 pints (a good 3 litres) water. The vegetables are plunged into boiling water, then blanched for a given length of time (see chart following) after the water has come back to a full boil. Thereafter the vegetables should be cooled rapidly, by plunging the basket into a large clean washing-up bowl of cold water. Then transfer the vegetables to a colander under cold running water.

Packaging and storing

Good packaging is essential and vegetables should be packed in suitable containers which are well labelled (see **Packaging for the freezer**). It is very important for vegetables that all air is excluded, and they should be packed in the most frequently used quantities as this saves wastage, and is more handy for mealtimes.

During prolonged storage there is a slight deterioration in flavour, texture, colour, and nutritional value, so the recommended storage time for most vegetables is 12 months.

VEGETABLE	PREPARATION FOR FREEZING	BLANCHING TIME	TO COOK AND USE
Artichoke (Globe)	Cut off stalk, remove outer leaves. Blanch few at a time. Tightly pack each in a polythene bag.	6 minutes (small) 8 minutes (large)	*Plunge frozen in boiling salted water for about 10 minutes until outer leaves can be removed easily.*
Artichoke (Jerusalem)	Cook and freeze as a purse in polythene containers.		*Thaw and use in soups.*
Asparagus	Grade into thick and thin stems. Cut in even lengths. Blanch, tie in convenient size bundles, then freeze in rigid containers.	2 minutes (thin) 4 minutes (thick)	*Plunge into boiling salted water for 3-5 minutes.*
Aubergines	Peel. Cut roughly into 1 inch (2.5 cm) slices. Blanch. Drain well. Open freeze. Pack in layers in polythene containers.	4 minutes	*Plunge frozen into boiling salted water for 5 minutes. Thaw before using for moussaka.*
Broad beans	Select young and tender beans. Shell and blanch. Pack in bags or polythene containers.	1 ½ minutes	*Plunge frozen into boiling salted water for 5-8 minutes.*
French beans	Top and tail, string. Grade and cut larger ones into 1 ½ inch (4cm) lengths. Blanch, then freeze in polythene bags.	1 ½ minutes	*Plunge frozen into boiling salted water. 3 minutes (cut) 5 minutes (whole)*
Runner beans	String. Top and tail. Slice into even ½ inch (1cm) diagonal slices. Blanch and freeze in polythene bags.	1 minute (first picking), or 2 minutes for mid season	*Plunge frozen into boiling salted water for about 3 minutes.*
Beetroot	Choose small beetroot. Twist off leaves leaving 1 inch (2.5cm) stalk to prevent bleeding. Cook until tender in boiling salted water. Peel then leave whole, slice or dice. Pack in polythene bags.		*Thaw in refrigerator up to 6 hours, depending on size.*

VEGETABLE	PREPARATION FOR FREEZING	BLANCHING TIME	TO COOK AND USE
Broccoli, Calabrese	Remove outer leaves, trim off woody stem. Grade into same size thickness of stem. Blanch. Pack in polythene containers.	2 minutes (thick) 1 minute (thin)	*Plunge frozen into boiling salted water for 5-8 minutes.*
Brussels sprouts	Trim. Grade. No need to cross bottoms of small ones. Blanch. Pack in polythene bags or containers.	1½ minutes (small) 3 minutes (medium)	*Plunge frozen into boiling salted water for 6-8 minutes.*
Cabbage	Use only young crisp cabbage. Shred coarsely. Blanch. Pack small quantities in polythene bags.	1 minute	*Plunge frozen into boiling salted water for 5 minutes.*
Carrots	Choose small whole carrots. Slice or dice larger ones. Blanch. Pack in polythene bags or containers.	3 minutes (small) 4 minutes (thick slices)	*Plunge frozen into boiling salted water for 5-15 minutes. Diced and sliced can be added frozen to casseroles.*
Cauliflower	Choose only firm white cauliflower. Break into florets. Blanch (lemon juice can be added to water to keep florets white). Pack in polythene bags or containers.	2 minutes	*Plunge frozen into boiling salted water for 5-8 minutes.*
Celeriac	Wash. Peel and dice. Blanch. Drain and pack in polythene bags *or* purée cooked celeriac in a blender. Cool, pack in polythene containers.	4 minutes	*Serve blanched celeriac boiled or sautéed in butter. Serve purée heated with butter and use for soup or as a vegetable mixed with mashed potato.*
Celery	Remove strings. Scrub well. Cut into ½ inch (1 cm) slices. Blanch. Pack in small quantities in polythene bags.	2 minutes	*Only suitable to add to cooked dishes, stews and casseroles.*
Chestnuts	Wash, cover with water and bring to boil. Drain and peel. Pack in rigid containers.	1-2 minutes	*Can supplement raw chestnuts in recipes. Can be cooked and frozen as a purée.*

VEGETABLE	PREPARATION FOR FREEZING	BLANCHING TIME	TO COOK AND USE
Chicory	Select fresh white heads. Trim. To keep colour add juice of ½ lemon to water for blanching. Pack in polythene bags.	3 minutes	*Only suitable for serving cooked. Plunge frozen into boiling salted water with 1 teaspoon sugar for about 10 minutes. Serve with a white sauce.*
Chillies	Remove stalks, scoop out seeds and pith. Blanch. Pack in polythene bags.	1 minute	*Add to casseroles.*
Corn on the cob	Select young, pale yellow kernels. Remove husks and silks. Blanch. Pack singly in polythene bags.	4-8 minutes according to size	*Thaw before cooking, otherwise inside still cold when corn cooked. When thawed boil in salted water for 5 minutes.*
Courgettes	Choose young even-sized courgettes. Cut in half if small or slice into 1 inch (2.5 cm) rounds. Blanch. Open freeze and pack in polythene bags.	1 minute	*Stir fry slices from frozen in butter and oil for 4 minutes or plunge into boiling salted water for 2 minutes.*
Fennel	Trim, cut into slices. Blanch. Pack in polythene bags.	3 minutes	*Only suitable for serving cooked. Add to stews or plunge into boiling salted water for 8 minutes. Serve with a cream sauce.*
Herbs	Chop herbs separately or mixed. Either pack in clean 1 oz (25 g) containers or ice trays. Cover with water. Freeze. Turn out cubes and pack in polythene bags.		*Keep colour but go limp on thawing. Good for flavour and bouquet garni.*
Kohlrabi	Choose small young roots. Trim, peel, leave small ones whole. Chop larger ones. Blanch. Pack in polythene bags.	2-4 minutes	*Plunge frozen into boiling salted water for 8-12 minutes.*

VEGETABLE	PREPARATION FOR FREEZING	BLANCHING TIME	TO COOK AND USE
Marrow	As courgettes, only bigger pieces. Remove skin. Blanch, then open freeze. Pack in polythene bags.	1 minute	*Plunge frozen into boiling salted water for about 3 minutes, or serve in a white sauce.*
Mushrooms	Use only fresh, cultivated mushrooms. Small ones are best. Slice if larger then button. Sauté in butter or freeze raw. Store 3 months cooked; 1 month raw. Pack in polythene bags.		*Add frozen to soups, casseroles and other dishes. Thaw raw mushrooms in the refrigerator.*
Onion	Peel, slice, chop or leave whole if small. Blanch. Label mild or strong. Pack in double thickness polythene bags. Not suitable for salads. Store up to 6 months.	2 minutes	*Add to soups, stews, casseroles, etc.*
Parsnips	Trim and peel. Leave small ones whole and cube larger ones. Blanch. Pack in polythene bags.	4 minutes (whole) 2 minutes (cubed)	*Plunge frozen into boiling salted water-about 15 minutes if whole, 10 minutes if cubed.*
Peas	Use only young peas. Pod and blanch. Pack in polythene bags or containers.	1 minute	*Plunge frozen into boiling salted water for 2-3 minutes.*
Peppers, red and green	Wash, remove stems, seeds and pith. Cut in half, strips or leave whole. Blanch and open freeze, then pack in polythene bags. Freeze red and green separately. Store up to 6 months.	3 minutes	*Use halved for stuffing, or add to dishes in strips from frozen.*
Potato croquettes	These freeze well. Make, then toss in breadcrumbs. Open freeze, pack in polythene containers.		*Thaw. Fry for about 4 minutes until golden brown.*
Chipped potatoes	Deep fry until tender but not brown. Cool quickly. Pack in polythene bags		*Thaw. Deep fry in small quantities*

VEGETABLE	PREPARATION FOR FREEZING	BLANCHING TIME	TO COOK AND USE
Duchesse pototaes	Open freeze. Pack in polythene containers. Store up to 3 months		*Thaw, glaze, brown at 400°F/200°C/Gas 6 for about 15 minutes.*
New potatoes	Use small even-sized potatoes. Cook fully with mint. Drain and cool with melted butter. Pack in polythene bags. Store for up to 6 months		*Thaw. Reheat in the melted butter.*
Roast potatoes	Slightly *under*-roast. Cool quickly. Pack in polythene bags. Store up to 6 months.		*Reheat from frozen in roasting tin for about 30 minutes until browned at 375°F/190°C/Gas 5.*
Leaf spinach	Blanch in small quantities, cool quickly and press out excess moisture. Pack in polythene bags.	1 minute	*Plunge frozen into boiling salted water for about 5 minutes. Drain well. Add butter.*
Tomatoes, whole	Freeze, but not suitable for salads. Pack in polythene bags.		*Thaw slightly for about 5 minutes, then the skins will slip off and the tomatoes can be added to casseroles.*
Tomato purée	Cooked and bought purée can be packed in small polythene containers or ice cube trays.		*Add to soups, casseroles etc.*
Turnips	Choose young roots. Prepare as for parsnips.	4 minutes (small) 2 minutes (cubed)	*Plunge frozen into boiling salted water for up to 10 minutes depending on size.*

Freezing fruit

Freezing is the best and easiest way of preserving fruit. The recommended storage time for frozen fruit is 12 months.

Choose only best quality, ripe, fresh fruit. If fruit is *over*-ripe often it can be puréed and frozen, for example raspberries and other soft fruit.

I use two methods of freezing fruit only—open freezing and syrup pack. I do not use dry sugar.

Open freezing method

There is no need to open freeze if fruit is dry and in peak condition, but if it is at all moist it should be open frozen. The aim is to freeze fruit until firm then to pack, so it remains in separate pieces. This makes it free flowing, easy for removing small amounts, and prevents squashing.

To open freeze, arrange fruit on trays without touching and freeze until firm. Freezing time will vary according to each fruit. It can take from 1 to 8 hours. Once solid the fruit can be packed in polythene bags or containers.

Syrup method

This is suitable for apricots, cherries, peaches, grapefruit, oranges, melon, plums, pears and pineapple. Some fruits discolour easily and need special treatment by sprinkling with lemon juice or adding ascorbic acid to the syrup in proportions of ¼ teaspoon of ascorbic acid to 1 pint (600ml) of water. These fruits are peaches, apricots, and light coloured cherries.

The strength of the syrup depends on how sweet you like your fruit.

% solution	sugar	water	strength
20%	4oz (100g)	1 pint (600ml)	thin
30%	7oz (200g)	1 pint (600ml)	medium
50%	1 lb (450g)	1 pint (600ml)	heavy

When making the syrup, dissolve the sugar in the water, then bring to boil without stirring. Remove from heat, and leave to cool thoroughly before pouring over prepared fruit.

Use ½ pint (300ml) syrup to every 1 lb (450g) of fruit. Choosing the strength of the syrup depends on whether the fruit flavour is delicate and may be overpowered by a strong syrup, or whether the fruit is sour and may be improved by a heavy syrup.

Cooked fruit

Apples, apricots, plums, damsons and pears can be stewed and frozen in quantities ready for pies, sauces and puddings, or just to serve as stewed fruit.

Fruit purées

Raw, ripe and over-ripe fruit such as apples, gooseberries, raspberries and blackberries can be puréed for sauces or used to flavour icecream, soufflés, mousses and fools.

Delicate fruits can be packed puréed without cooking, but usually fruits are puréed using the minimum of water, about 4 tablespoons to each 1 lb (450g) of fruit. Cook fruit to a pulp over gentle heat. Purée in a processor for speed then, if the fruit has pips, pass through a sieve (gooseberries, blackberries, blackcurrants and raspberries). Cool quickly and pack in containers. The size of containers can vary with the intended use of the purée; it is a good idea, for example, to pack small cartons of apple purée to use in a sauce. I use clean cream cartons, 5 oz (150g) for two people, and the 10 oz (275g) size for four.

Puréed fruits take up a lot less space in the freezer than whole fruits, and are quick and easy to use after thawing.

Packaging

In purée form, use old, clean 5 oz (150g) and 10 oz (275g) cream and yoghurt pots, as above. Old, clean icecream boxes are the most useful for larger quantities of previously open frozen fruits.

Thawing

If fruit is to be cooked, thaw at room temperature until the fruits separate individually. Cook gently to prevent fruit breaking up.

If the fruit is to be served raw, thaw slowly in container in the fridge. Most fruits are best cold and slightly frozen: strawberries and raspberries, for example, tend to become soft if thawed for too long.

It takes about 6 hours to thaw 1 lb (450g) of fruit.

If fruit to be used for marmalade or jam making is not thawed first it will give a better colour. Turn into preserving pan, add usual amount of water, and simmer until tender, as per recipe. When using frozen oranges for marmalade choose the whole fruit method.

FRUIT	PREPARATION FOR FREEZER	USE AFTER FREEZING
Apples	Peel, core and slice into cold salted water to prevent browning, then rinse before cooking. Stew until tender in minimum water, add 2-4 oz (50-100g) sugar per 1 lb (450g) to taste. Cool and pack in polythene containers.	*Stewed, in pie fillings, crumbles.*
	Or, for a *purée*, stew until tender with minimum water and add 2 oz (50g) sugar. Process or sieve. Cool and pack in small clean containers.	*Puréed, in apple sauce, baby foods.*
Apricots	*In syrup.* Wash, halve and stone. Pack in syrup with ascorbic acid in polythene containers. Can be left whole but develop an almond flavour around the stone with time. *Stewed,* as apple but stoned. *Purée,* as apple but stoned.	*For serving cold as a dessert or in fruit salads.* *Dessert.* *For icecream, flavouring and sauces.*
Avocado pears	Not very satisfactory. Only freeze as purée, as they lose texture if frozen whole. Remove stone. Scoop out flesh, mash with 1 tablespoon lemon juice, per pear. Pack in small polythene containers. Storage up to 3 months.	*For avocado dips, sandwich fillings and soups.*
Bananas	Not very satisfactory. Best to use mushy bananas in a banana cake and freeze that. Do not freeze as whole fruit. Can be puréed by mashing or in a processor. Add juice of 1 lemon or 2 tablespoons sugar to each 1 lb (450g). Pack in rigid container.	*Use for sandwich filling, in banana cakes or loaves.*
Bilberries	Freeze dry in plastic containers.	*Use in pies or tarts.*
Blackberries	Choose firm, ripe fruit. Pick on a dry day, wash only if necessary, drain thoroughly and hull. If dry pack in polythene containers. If damp open freeze. Can be cooked, *puréed*, then sieved.	*Use for jam and jelly making, and any kind of pudding or sauce.* *Use purée for sauces, mousse, icecream flavouring.*
Blackcurrants, blueberries and redcurrants	Choose ripe firm currants, remove stalks. Wash only if necessary and dry thoroughly. Pack in polythene containers. To purée, stew 6 oz (175g) sugar to 1 lb (450g) fruit, then process, sieve and pack in polythene containers.	*Use in jam making. Serve in pies, puddings, crumbles or as stewed currants. Use whole in fruit salads and to flavour icecreams and fruit drinks.*

FRUIT	PREPARATION FOR FREEZER	USE AFTER FREEZING
Cherries	Choose ripe, sweet cherries. Red freeze better than black. Remove stones if liked; if left in may get slight almond flavour after 6 months. Open freeze or dry pack in rigid containers. Light coloured cherries can be covered with a cold 50% strength syrup and ascorbic acid. Leave a head space.	*Use in pies, flans and pudding. For icecream topping, add a little Kirsch after cooking and cooling.*
Coconut	Shred on a coarse grater. Add coconut milk and pack in polythene containers.	*When using pour off the milk, and drink or use. Shreds can b toasted.*
Crab apples	If no time to make crab apple jelly, cook fruit and strain juice. Measure and freeze the juice to make jelly another day. Store in ½ pint (300ml) cream pots for up to 6 months.	*Crab apple jelly.*
Cranberries	Treat as other berries, and freeze in polythene containers.	*To make sauce, jelly or in pies.*
Damsons	Wash, and *stew* or *purée*. Store in containers.	*Use as a purée or as a stewed fruit for pies and puddings.*
Figs	Either peel and pack in a cold 30% syrup or leave whole and wrap in foil to use as dessert figs (not very satisfactory as they lose texture).	*In a syrup as a dessert with cream or in a green fruit salad.*
Gooseberries	Top and tail and pack whole, dry and fresh in polythene bags. *Stew* with 4-6 oz (100-175g) sugar to 1 lb (450g) fruit. Reduce to a *purée*, sieve and pack in small containers.	*Use whole for jam making, pies, or crumbles. Use purée fo fools and icecream.*
Grapefruit	Peel, remove pips and pith, segment. Freeze with or without sugar syrup in rigid containers.	*Use for adding to fruit salads, as a starter, or a dessert with added liquor after thawing.*
Grapes	Seedless can be packed whole, others should be halved and pipped. Pack in a 30% strength cold syrup.	*For use in fruit salads or whol to incorporate in sauce for Sol Véronique.*

FRUIT	PREPARATION FOR FREEZER	USE AFTER FREEZING
Greengages	Halve, pack in rigid containers with 40% strength syrup with added ascorbic acid.	*Use in pies and puddings.*
Lemons and limes	1. Squeeze juice and freeze in ice-cube trays. 2. Leave whole, slice or segment before freezing. 3. To freeze the zest, peel with a potato peeler and cut rind into julienne strips. Blanch for 1 minute, and cool.	*Use as lemon juice.* *Use as lemons—give more juice if frozen.* *Use for garnishing or for marmalade.*
Loganberries	Wash only if necessary. Dry thoroughly. Pack in small quantities in containers. Open freeze first if at all damp.	*For puddings and sauces.*
Mangoes	Peel and slice ripe fruit into a cold 30% syrup. Add 2 tablespoons of lemon juice to each 2 pints (1.2 litres) of syrup. Store in containers.	*Serve with additional lemon juice and serve ice cold as a dessert.*
Melons (Cantaloupe, Galia, Honeydew)	Peel, remove pips and pith. Slice, freeze in syrup. Store in containers.	*Use for adding to fruit salad or serving alone.*
Oranges (sweet)	Peel, remove pith and pips, slice. Freeze in syrup. Juice can be frozen in ice-cube trays and packed in polythene bags.	*Use in fruit salads or serve alone. Add liqueur after thawing if liked.*
Oranges (bitter, Seville)	Freeze whole. Pack in polythene bags and label giving weight.	*Use for marmalade.*
Peaches and nectarines	Blanch for 1 minute. Lift off skin, cut in half or into slices. Poach in 30% syrup for 2 minutes. Drain and cool. Add ¼ teaspoon ascorbic acid to 1 pint (600ml) cold syrup. Pour over fruit. As fruit tends to float, cover first with a piece of crumpled greaseproof paper before packing in polythene containers.	*Serve ice-cold as a dessert. For special occasions add brandy after thawing.*

FRUIT	PREPARATION FOR FREEZER	USE AFTER FREEZING
Pears	Don't freeze well as delicate flavour. Best frozen in blackberry or raspberry syrup. Peel, core and slice. Poach in a 30% boiling syrup for 2 minutes then cool. Add 2 tablespoons blackberry or raspberry purée to ½ pint (300ml) syrup. Pour over fruit and pack in polythene containers.	*Serve alone or in puddings and fruit salads.*
Pineapple	Peel and core, then slice, dice or crush. Open freeze or freeze in syrup. Pack in rigid containers.	*Use in fruit salad or for adding to cream for gateaux, etc.*
Plums	Wash if necessary. Dry. 1. Cut in half, remove stones, cover with 50% syrup and pack in polythene containers. 2. Leave whole and pack in polythene bags.	*Pies, crumbles and puddings.* *Jam making.*
Raspberries	Wash only if absolutely necessary. 1. Open freeze if damp then pack in containers. 2. Pack in small polythene containers. 3. *Purée*, then pack in polythene containers or ice-cube trays.	*} Serve with cream.* *Use in soufflés, sorbets and mousses.*
Rhubarb	Cut off green. Wash and dry. Cut into ¾ inch (2 cm) lengths. 1. Pack straight in polythene bags. 2. *Blanch* for 1 minute to retain colour, pack in polythene containers.	*Use for stewed rhubarb, pies and crumbles.*
Strawberries	1. Open freeze if damp then pack in polythene containers. 2. Pack in small polythene containers. 3. *Purée* or *sieve* then pack in small containers.	*Fruit salad or serving with cream.* *Mousses, sorbet and icecream.*

SOUPS

AND STARTERS

One of the things I find most useful to have in the freezer is good strong bone stock ready to use for soups and sauces. I reduce it considerably by boiling before freezing it so that it takes up less room in the freezer. Then I pour it into sparkling clean ½ pint (300ml) cream cartons and freeze until solid. Take care to balance the cartons very carefully so they don't spill before they freeze. I don't bother to put lids on the cartons unless I happen to have the clip-on type.

If you are in a hurry you can take soup straight from the freezer and thaw slowly in a non-stick pan—it's best to put a little water in the bottom of the pan first to stop the soup sticking. It is very handy to have masses of croûtons in the freezer to cheer up soup and make it more filling. They take no time to thaw—5 minutes in the oven or a couple of minutes under the grill is enough.

Gazpacho

Make when tomatoes are really cheap in late summer. Be sure to choose ripe ones.

serves 4

1 lb (450g) tomatoes, skinned and sliced
1 small onion, sliced
1 fat clove garlic, crushed
2 slices white bread, crusts removed
4 tablespoons white wine vinegar
5 tablespoons vegetable oil
½ pint (300ml) chicken stock
2 oz (50g) green pepper, very finely diced
juice of ½ lemon
salt
freshly ground black pepper

for serving only
3 oz (75g) cucumber, diced

Put the tomatoes, onion, garlic, bread, vinegar, oil and stock in a processor or blender and process for a few seconds until the mixture is well blended. Turn the mixture into a bowl, then stir in the green pepper, lemon juice and seasoning.

to freeze   Turn into a rigid container, cover, label and freeze.

to thaw   Thaw overnight in the refrigerator. Serve with the diced cucumber.

Carrot and Orange Soup

Use orange juice from a carton, the kind you have for breakfast and keep in the refrigerator. No need to add the cream if you like it less rich.

serves 6

2 oz (50g) butter
8 oz (225g) onion, finely chopped
2 lb (900g) carrots, sliced
1 pint (600ml) orange juice
salt
freshly ground black pepper
1 pint (600ml) chicken stock

for serving only
¼ pint (150ml) double cream
2 tablespoons snipped chives

Heat the butter in a pan and fry onion until soft but not brown, then tip into a processor or blender. Cook the carrots in boiling salted water for about 15 minutes until just tender, drain and add to the onion. Add orange juice and seasoning to the blender, then process until smooth. Mix with the stock.

to serve now
Stir in cream and chives just before serving, either very cold or piping hot.

to freeze
Freeze in a rigid container before adding cream and chives, seal, and label.

to thaw
Thaw in the refrigerator overnight and serve as above.

Cream of Artichoke Soup

Artichoke soup is delicious and freezes well. It is always better to peel the artichokes after cooling; they're so knobbly!

serves 6

2 lb (900g) Jerusalem artichokes
1 oz (25g) butter
1 ½ pint (scant litre) chicken stock
salt
freshly ground black pepper

for serving only
½ pint (300ml) milk
cream

Put the artichokes in a pan and cover with cold water. Bring to the boil, cover and simmer for about 15 minutes, then drain well and peel. Rinse out the pan and melt the butter in it; add the artichokes, stock and seasoning. Cover and simmer for about 30 minutes. Purée in a processor or blender.

to freeze Turn into a rigid container before adding milk and cream. Cool, cover, label and freeze.

to thaw Thaw at room temperature for about 8 hours. Reheat in a pan with the milk. Bring to the boil then serve each plate garnished with a swirl of cream.

Cream of Mushroom Soup

Mushrooms can often be bought very cheaply from the greengrocers at the end of the day. This is an ideal way of serving them—or those mushroom stalks sometimes sold by themselves, or saved from other recipes.

serves 4-6
2oz (50g) butter
4 oz (100g) onion, chopped
8 oz (225g) mushrooms, chopped
2 oz (50g) flour
1¼ pints (750ml) good chicken stock
salt
freshly ground black pepper

for serving only
½ pint (300ml) milk

Melt the butter in a pan, add the onion and fry gently for about 5 minutes until beginning to soften. Add the mushrooms and continue to cook for a further 5 minutes. Add the flour and cook for a minute, then gradually blend in the stock, stirring until thickened. Season well with salt and pepper and simmer gently for about 10 minutes.

to serve now   Stir in the milk, bring to the boil and serve.

to freeze now   Turn into a rigid container, allow to cool, then cover, seal, label and freeze.

to thaw   Thaw at room temperature for about 5 hours then turn into a pan, reheat gently then stir in the milk as above.

Potato and Leek Soup

A delicious soup which is simple to make.

serves 6

1 lb (450g) potatoes, peeled and diced
1 lb (450g) leeks, finely sliced
sprig of fresh thyme
1 bayleaf
1 teaspoon salt
¾ pint (450ml) water

for serving only
1 oz (25g) butter
1 oz (25g) flour
1 pint (600ml) milk
freshly ground black pepper

Put the prepared vegetables, thyme and bayleaf in a pan with salt and water. Bring to the boil and simmer for about 20 minutes until tender. Remove and discard herbs then reduce vegetables and water to a purée in a processor or blender.

to serve now
Melt butter in a pan, stir in flour and cook 1 minute, gradually blending in the milk. Stir continuously until thickened, then stir in seasoning and purée. Bring to the boil and serve.

to freeze
Freeze cooled *purée only* in a rigid container, seal and label.

to thaw
Thaw purée at room temperature for about 6 hours, then make up with milk as above.

Green Pepper and Onion Soup

Such a good soup. It is essential to sieve it after puréeing as you need to get rid of the fine pieces of pepper skin. The soup is smooth after puréeing, so it is not a chore, and the soup runs through the sieve easily, leaving the skin behind.

---

serves 6

2oz (50g) butter
2 tablespoons sunflower oil
8 oz (225g) green pepper, seeded, cored and diced
1 lb (450g) onions, chopped
1½oz (40g) flour
¾ pint (450ml) chicken stock

for serving only
¾ pint (450ml) milk
salt
freshly ground black pepper
croûtons (see page 43)

Heat the butter and oil in a saucepan, add the green pepper and onions, and cook gently for 5 minutes, until the vegetables are soft. Blend in the flour and cook for 1 minute. Gradually stir in the stock, bring to the boil, and then simmer for 30 minutes until the vegetables are cooked.

Pour the soup into a processor or blender and process until smooth, then sieve.

to serve now

Rinse out the pan and return the soup to it. Stir in the milk and bring to the boil, taste and check seasoning. Serve garnished with croûtons.

to freeze

Before adding milk, turn into a rigid container, cool, cover, label and freeze.

to thaw

Thaw at room temperature for about 6 hours. Heat in a pan with the milk, stirring continuously. Serve as above.

Tomato and Beetroot Borsch

This is a delicious, and tasty, hot version of the famous Russian soup.

serves 6-8

1 tablespoon bacon fat
1 large onion, chopped
14 oz (397g) can tomatoes
8 oz (225g) cooked beetroot, diced
1 ½ pints (900ml) chicken stock
1 tablespoon white wine vinegar
1 tablespoon caster sugar
salt
freshly ground black pepper

for serving only
a few snipped chives
3 teaspoons strong horseradish sauce
5 oz (15g) carton soured cream

Measure the fat into a frying pan then fry the chopped onion until pale golden. Add tomatoes, beetroot, stock, vinegar, sugar and seasoning. Simmer 10-15 minutes without a lid. Check seasoning then reduce to a purée in a processor or blender.

to serve now

Bring just to the boil, and do not simmer long as its colour will fade. Serve with snipped chives, and a horseradish cream made simply by mixing the horseradish sauce and soured cream together.

to freeze

Allow to cool then pack in a rigid container, cover, seal, label and freeze.

to thaw

Thaw overnight in the refrigerator then heat through in a pan and serve as above.

Chicken and Onion Soup

A good family soup. The sugar helps to brown the onions quickly.

serves 8

2 oz (50g) butter
1 ½ lb (675g) onions, chopped
2 teaspoons caster sugar
1 ½ oz (40g) flour
*3 pints (1.7 litres) home-made chicken stock, plus bits of chicken picked
    off carcass*
salt
freshly ground black pepper

Melt butter in a large pan and gently fry onions with sugar for about 10 minutes until golden brown. Stir in flour and cook for 1 minute, then gradually blend in stock, stirring until boiling point is reached. Stir in the chicken bits, reduce heat and simmer gently for about 30 minutes. Season to taste.

to freeze   Allow to cool then pour into a rigid container, seal, label and freeze.

to thaw   Thaw at room temperature for about 8 hours, then reheat in a pan until piping hot and serve.

Tomato Soup

Always a favourite with the children.

serves 3
1 oz (25g) butter
4 oz (100g) onion, finely chopped
1 oz (25g) flour
½ pint (300ml) water
2½ oz (62g) can tomato purée

for serving only
½ pint (300ml) milk
1 teaspoon caster sugar
salt
freshly ground black pepper
Parmesan cheese, grated
freshly chopped parsley

Melt the butter in a pan, add the onion and fry gently for about 5 minutes until beginning to soften but not colour. Stir in the flour and cook for a minute. Remove from the heat and gradually blend in the water and tomato purée. Return to the heat and bring to the boil, stirring.

to serve now Stir in the milk, sugar and seasoning. Bring back to the boil then pour into bowls, sprinkle with cheese and parsley, and serve at once.

to freeze Turn into a rigid container, seal, label and freeze.

to thaw Thaw at room temperature for about 5 hours then turn into a pan. Reheat, then stir in the milk, sugar and seasoning, etc. as above.

Watercress Soup

Use the very best pieces of watercress for garnish or for a salad, and use stalks and less beautiful leaves in this delicious soup.

serves 6

2 bunches watercress
2 oz (50g) butter
1 onion, peeled and sliced
12 oz (350g) potatoes, peeled and sliced
1 pint (600ml) chicken stock
salt
freshly ground black pepper

for serving only
¾ pint (450ml) milk
¼ pint (150ml) single cream

Wash watercress but do not remove the stalks. Melt the butter in a pan and gently cook the onion and potato for 5 minutes without browning. Add the stock and seasoning, bring to the boil, then cover and simmer for about 15 minutes. Add watercress, and simmer for a further 10 minutes then purée in a processor or blender.

to serve now

Return puréed soup to pan, stir in milk and heat through. Stir in cream just before serving.

to freeze

Freeze before adding milk and cream. Pour into a rigid container, cool, cover, label and freeze.

to thaw

Thaw overnight in the refrigerator, turn into a pan, heat, and add milk and cream as above.

Courgette Soup

In mid summer courgettes are most plentiful and at their best.

serves 6

2oz (50g) butter
1 small onion, finely chopped
1½ lb (675g) courgettes, coarsely grated
1½oz (40g) flour
¾ pint (450 ml) good chicken stock

for serving only
¾ pint (450ml) milk
a little grated nutmeg
salt
freshly ground black pepper

Melt the butter in a large pan and quickly sauté the onion for about 5 minutes until golden brown, then add courgettes and fry until they begin to soften. Stir in flour and cook for 2 minutes then gradually blend in the stock and bring to the boil, stirring, until thickened.

to serve now
Stir in the milk, nutmeg and seasoning, and bring back to the boil. Cover and simmer gently for about 20 minutes then taste and check seasoning.

to freeze
Turn into a rigid container, cover, seal, label and freeze.

to thaw
Thaw at room temperature for about 6 hours, then turn into a pan, add milk, etc. as above, and reheat gently until piping hot.

Spiced Apple Soup

A rather unusual soup but the apple flavour is delicious.

serves 6

3 oz (75g) butter
4 oz (100g) onion, chopped
1½ lb (675g) Bramley apples, peeled, cored and chopped
1 fat clove garlic, crushed
1 oz (25g) flour
1 rounded teaspoon curry powder
2 pints (1.2 litres) good chicken stock
salt
freshly ground black pepper

for serving only
¼ pint (150ml) crème fraîche
snipped chives

Melt the butter in a large pan, add the onion, apple and garlic and fry gently for about 5 minutes until beginning to soften. Stir in the flour and curry powder and cook for a minute, blend in the stock and bring to the boil, stirring. Cover and simmer gently for about 20 minutes until the onion is tender.

Either sieve the soup, or process it in a processor or blender until smooth.

to serve now
Reheat until piping hot. Stir in the crème fraîche, taste and check seasoning, and sprinkle with chives just before serving.

to freeze
Turn into a rigid container, allow to cool, cover, seal, label and freeze.

to thaw
Thaw at room temperature for about 5 hours then turn into a pan and reheat. Add cream and chives as above.

Mild Curried Parsnip Soup

A really good soup, this is well worth making when parsnips are at their best and cheapest.

serves 6

3 oz (75g) butter
4 oz (100g) onion, chopped
1 lb (450g) parsnips, cubed
1 fat clove garlic, crushed
1 oz (25g) flour
1 rounded teaspoon curry powder
2 pints (1.2 litres) good beef stock
salt
freshly ground black pepper

for serving only
¼ pint (150ml) single cream
snipped chives

Melt the butter in a large pan, add the onion, parsnip and garlic, and fry gently for about 5 minutes. Stir in the flour and curry powder and cook for a minute, then blend in the stock and seasoning. Bring to the boil, stirring, then cover and simmer gently for about 20 minutes until the parsnip is tender. Sieve the soup, or process in a processor or blender until smooth.

to serve now

Reheat until piping hot, taste and check seasoning. Stir in the cream just before serving, and sprinkle chives on top.

to freeze

Turn into a rigid container, allow to cool then cover, label and freeze.

to thaw

Thaw at room temperature for about 5 hours then turn into a pan and reheat and garnish as above.

French Onion Soup

A delicious soup for when it is cold and wintry outside.

serves 4
3 tablespoons sunflower oil
1 lb (450g) onions, finely chopped
2 teaspoons sugar
1 oz (25g) flour
2 pints (1.2 litres) good beef stock
salt
freshly ground black pepper

for serving only
4 slices French bread
2 oz (50g) well flavoured Cheddar cheese

Heat the oil in a large pan, add the onions and sugar and fry gently for about 10 minutes until golden brown. Stir occasionally to prevent them from sticking: they should not burn as this gives the soup a rather bitter taste. Stir in the flour and cook for a minute, then blend in the stock and bring to the boil, stirring. Add seasoning, cover with a lid and simmer for about 20 minutes.

to serve now
Taste and check seasoning. Toast French bread on one side, then sprinkle the cheese on the untoasted side and put under the grill until melted. Put a slice of the bread in the bottom of each soup bowl and pour soup over the bread. Serve immediately.

to freeze
Cool, turn into a rigid container, cover, label and freeze.

to thaw
Thaw at room temperature for about 6 hours then turn into a pan and reheat until lovely and hot, then proceed as above.

Scotch Broth

Very warming in winter and inexpensive to make too. This quantity could be frozen in separate containers, to serve more than one meal.

**makes
5 pints
(2.8 litres)**

*4 oz (100g) dry soup mix
   or 1 ½ oz (40g) pearl barley
   1 oz (25g) dried peas
   1 oz (25g) dried lentils
1 ½ lb (675g) scrag end of neck of lamb, jointed
5 pints (2.8 litres) water
salt
freshly ground black pepper
1 ½ lb (675g) chopped vegetables
   (including onion, leek, carrots and a little swede)*

for serving only
1 good tablespoon chopped parsley

Soak dry soup mix or barley, peas and lentils in a bowl of water overnight.

Trim surplus fat off the lamb and discard. Put lamb in a large pan with water, seasoning and strained dried vegetables. Bring to boil, cover and simmer for an hour then add freshly chopped vegetables, and cook for a further hour. Lift out the lamb, remove all the meat, cut into small pieces and return to pan. Discard bones. Check seasoning.

to freeze
Allow to cool then pour into rigid containers, cover, seal, label and freeze.

to thaw
Thaw at room temperature for about 6 hours then reheat in a pan and serve with chopped parsley sprinkled on top.

French Pea Soup with Croûtons

A quick and easy soup made from frozen peas. Serve with croûtons which you will have in your 'store-cupboard' freezer. Make a whole loaf's worth of croûtons at a time.

serves 6

1 oz (25g) butter
3 shallots, chopped
12 large lettuce leaves, roughly shredded
1 lb (450g) frozen peas
1¾ pints (1 litre) chicken stock
salt
freshly ground black pepper

Melt the butter in a pan, add shallots and lettuce and cook for 2 minutes. Add the peas, stock and seasoning, bring to the boil and simmer gently for about 5 minutes. Sieve or purée in a processor or blender.

to freeze Turn into a rigid container, cool, cover, label and freeze.

to thaw Thaw overnight in the refrigerator. Reheat gently in a pan, taste and adjust seasoning.

Croûtons

1 loaf day-old sliced bread
oil for frying

Cut bread into pencil-sized strips, then cut again to form cubes. Deep fry until golden brown, lift out with a slotted spoon and drain on kitchen paper.

to freeze Store in freezer in a large polythene bag.

to thaw Take out the required amount of croûtons, and reheat in a warm oven until crisp.

Soup Accompaniments

Both the following are easy, are so useful to have in the freezer, and transform the simplest of soups! See also croûtons on the previous page.

Garlic Herb Loaf

2 cloves garlic
salt
freshly ground black pepper
4 oz (100g) soft butter
1 teaspoon freshly chopped mixed herbs
1 teaspoon freshly chopped parsley
1 French loaf

Crush the garlic and put in a bowl with the salt, pepper, butter and herbs. Cream well. Cut the loaf along in 1 inch (2.5 cm) slices to within ½ inch (1.5 cm) of the bottom. Spread the slices on each side with the garlic butter and press together again. Wrap in foil.

to freeze   Label and freeze, very tightly over-wrapped with foil or in a poly bag.

to thaw   Thaw at room temperature for 3-4 hours, then heat in the oven at 400°F/200°C/Gas 6 for about 15 minutes, still in foil, until hot and crisp.

Cheese Toasties

1 oz (25g) soft butter
1 fat clove garlic, crushed
2 oz (50g) Cheddar cheese, grated
4 thick slices French bread

Cream the butter and garlic then mix with the cheese. Spread over the slices of bread.

to freeze   Open freeze, then wrap in foil interleaved with greaseproof paper, and return to the freezer.

to thaw   Thaw for about 2 hours at room temperature then grill under a hot grill until golden brown.

Refreshing Starters

Try the melon and lime before a steak or a grill, and the orange water ice is delicious when served before a substantial main course.

Melon and Lime

serves 4

1 small Galia melon
juice of 1 lime
1 glass dry white wine
1 level tablespoon caster sugar

Halve the melon and remove the seeds. Peel the melon halves and cut flesh into cubes and place in a rigid container with the remaining ingredients. Leave to stand 1 hour.

to freeze

Cover, label and freeze.

to thaw

Thaw in the refrigerator overnight. Serve in wine glasses.

Orange Water Ice

serves 6

4 oz (100g) caster sugar
½ pint (300ml) water
6 oz (175g) can frozen concentrated orange juice, thawed
3 egg whites

for serving only
a few sprigs fresh mint

Dissolve the sugar in the water in a pan over gentle heat and allow to cool. Blend the orange juice with the sugar syrup then pour into a shallow polythene container. Freeze for about 45 minutes until just beginning to set.

Turn orange mixture into a bowl and mash until smooth. Whisk the egg whites with a hand-held electric or rotary whisk until stiff then fold into the orange mixture. Return to the container, cover and freeze.

to thaw

Thaw in the refrigerator for about 30 minutes then serve in scoopfuls in glass dishes garnished with mint sprigs.

Scallops with Mushrooms

When you buy scallops from the fishmonger, ask for some of the deep scallop shells so that you can use them as attractive serving dishes.

serves 4-6

6 scallops, black thread removed
¼ pint (150ml) cider
2 oz (50g) butter
2 oz (50g) flour
¾ pint (450ml) milk
2 oz (50g) well flavoured Cheddar cheese, grated
salt
freshly ground black pepper
2 oz (50g) small button mushrooms, sliced
mashed potato made with 1½ lb (675g) potatoes with 1 egg, a little milk
    and butter added

Rinse and slice the scallops; leave the coral whole. Put scallops in a pan with the cider, simmer for about 5 minutes, then drain, keeping the liquor on one side. Melt the butter, add the flour and cook for a minute. Stir in the cider liquor and milk, and bring to the boil, stirring. Add the cheese, scallops, seasoning and mushrooms.

Pipe the mashed potato in a border around 4 to 6 scallop shells or small ovenproof dishes, then spoon fish sauce in middle.

to freeze

Open freeze, then pack in polythene bags, seal and label and return to the freezer.

to thaw

Take from the freezer, remove bags and either cook at once in a hot oven (425°F/220°C/Gas 7) for about 1 hour, or thaw in the refrigerator for about 8 hours and then cook in the oven for about 15 minutes.

Plaice Florentine

This is an unusual dish in that the fish is not cooked before the dish is assembled. This ensures that the fish is not overcooked.

serves 8

8 small fillets of plaice, skinned
salt
freshly ground black pepper
juice of ½ lemon
2 oz (50g) butter
2 oz (50g) flour
1 pint (600ml) milk
1 lb (450g) frozen cut leaf spinach (cook as directed on the packet)
2 oz (50g) Cheddar cheese, grated
2 oz (25g) fresh white breadcrumbs

Season the fillets well with salt, pepper and lemon juice and roll up. Melt the butter in a small saucepan, add the flour and cook for a minute. Stir in the milk and bring to the boil, stirring until thickened. Simmer for about 2 minutes and season well. Blend 6 tablespoons of the sauce with the spinach and place in a 2 pint (1.2 litre) ovenproof dish. Arrange the fish on top and spoon over the remaining sauce. Mix the cheese and breadcrumbs together and sprinkle on top of the sauce.

to freeze   Cover with foil, label and freeze.

to thaw   Thaw at room temperature for about 6 hours. Heat the oven to 400°F/200°C/Gas 6. Remove the foil and cook in the oven for about 20 minutes until the top is a pale golden brown and the fish white.

Mushroom Mousse

This mousse freezes well for a short time; if frozen longer than 10 days it shrinks a little and the mushrooms make it watery. Serve with French dressed mushrooms (which you should *not* freeze).

serves 10-12

½ oz (15g) powdered gelatine
4 tablespoons cold water
10 oz (275g) can condensed consommé
2 oz (50g) butter
8 oz (225g) button mushrooms
½ pint (300ml) whipping cream, whipped
½ pint (300ml) good mayonnaise
½ teaspoon curry powder
salt and freshly ground black pepper

French dressed mushrooms, for serving only
8 oz (225g) button mushrooms
½ clove garlic, crushed
½ teaspoon dry mustard
salt and freshly ground black pepper
1 teaspoon caster sugar
1¼ pint (150 ml) sunflower oil
4-6 tablespoons white wine vinegar

Put gelatine in a small bowl with the water, and leave for about 3 minutes to form a sponge. Stand in a pan of simmering water until the gelatine is clear, then remove from heat and cool. Add to consommé.

Melt butter in a pan and fry mushrooms for about 5 minutes until tender. Allow to cool then chop finely (less colour is lost this way). Mix together the chopped mushrooms, cream, mayonnaise and curry powder and when the consommé is cold and thick but not set, blend into the mayonnaise mixture. Add seasoning then pour into an oiled 2 pint (1.2 litre) ring mould. Chill until set.

to serve now

Prepare French dressed mushrooms. Wipe the button mushrooms, trim the stalks level with the caps and slice very finely. Put in a bowl. Blend all remaining ingredients except the vinegar together in a bowl and then gradually mix in the vinegar. Pour dressing over mushrooms and toss well. Cover and chill for 2 hours before serving with the mousse.

to freeze

Cover mousse mould with foil, seal, label and freeze for up to 10 days.

to thaw

Thaw in the refrigerator overnight. Turn out of mould and serve.

Cucumber Mousse

A deliciously light mousse which freezes well for up to 10 days.

serves 8
1 cucumber, peeled, seeded and diced
salt
½ oz (15g) gelatine
3 tablespoons water
¼ pint (150ml) good chicken stock
8 oz (225g) cream cheese
juice of ½ lemon
¼ pint (150ml) mayonnaise
½ pint (300ml) whipping cream, whipped
freshly ground black pepper
2 tablespoons snipped chives

for serving only
bunch of watercress

Put the cucumber on a plate, sprinkle with salt and leave for about an hour until juices have run. Rinse well under running cold water, then drain thoroughly on kitchen paper.

Put the gelatine in a small bowl, add the water and leave for about 3 minutes to form a sponge. Stand the bowl in a pan of simmering water until gelatine has dissolved, and become a clear liquid. Allow to cool, then stir into the stock.

Put the cream cheese in a bowl and beat until smooth then stir in the cucumber and all the remaining ingredients, adding the stock last of all. Taste and check seasoning then pour into a lightly greased 1½ pint (900ml) ring mould. Chill in the refrigerator until set

to freeze Cover mould with foil, seal, label and freeze.

to thaw Thaw in the refrigerator overnight. Turn mousse out of mould and serve on a bed of watercress.

Smoked Salmon Mousse

If you can get smoked salmon pieces this is a very good way of making the most of them for a special occasion. You really do need a processor or blender for this recipe, which freezes well for up to 2 weeks.

To freeze or serve, the mousse needs to be turned out of the mould. If difficult, stand mould in a bowl of hot water for a couple of seconds. Take care not to leave it in the water too long or it will start to melt!

serves 10
½ oz (15g) packet powdered gelatine
3 tablespoons cold water
¼ pint (150 ml) chicken stock
juice of ½ lemon
½ pint (300ml) home-made or good bought mayonnaise
¼ pint (150ml) double cream, lightly whipped
8 oz (225g) cream cheese
a little salt and freshly ground black pepper
2 good tablespoons tomato purée
8 oz (225g) smoked salmon pieces

for serving only
1 bunch watercress
a few whole prawns in their shells

Put the gelatine in a small bowl with the cold water and stand for 3 minutes, then put in a pan of simmering water and dissolve until the gelatine has become clear. Remove and leave to cool.

Put all the other ingredients in a processor or blender and process until smooth then mix in the gelatine. Pour the mixture into a 2½ pint (1.4 litre) ring mould or dish and chill in the refrigerator until set (about 4 hours).

to serve now
Turn out of mould on to serving plate. Fill the centre of the ring with watercress and decorate with prawns. Serve with brown bread and butter.

to freeze
Turn out of mould and open freeze on a tray. Wrap in cling film and put in a polythene bag then return to the freezer.

to thaw
Remove wrapping, put on the serving plate, and thaw in the refrigerator for about 12 hours. Serve as above.

Smoked Salmon Pâté

Salmon pieces may often be bought at the end of a busy day at the delicatessen counter—they are the last cuts from a side of salmon, and are most reasonable. Sometimes they can be ordered ahead and then frozen until needed.

serves 6 as a first course

8 oz (225g) smoked salmon pieces
9 oz (250g) butter, just melted
juice of ½ lemon
freshly ground black pepper

Put fish and 8 oz (225g) of the butter in a processor or blender with remaining ingredients. Process until just smooth then spoon into a small pâté terrine. Level the top, pour remaining butter over pâté, and chill in the refrigerator until firm.

to freeze   Freeze in serving dish, wrapped with foil, sealed and labelled.

to thaw   Thaw overnight in the refrigerator before serving, with hot toast and butter.

Kipper Pâté

This pâté looks and tastes lovely served in individual ramekin dishes, garnished with slices of stuffed olives and served with hot granary toast.

serves 6

10 oz (283g) packet buttered kipper fillets
½ pint (300ml) whipping cream
juice of ½ lemon
pinch cayenne pepper

Cook the kipper fillets as directed on the packet, then remove them from the bag. Drain off and keep the butter.

Peel off and discard all the dark skin from the fillets then put them in a processor or blender with the cream, lemon juice, reserved butter and cayenne pepper. Process until smooth then taste and check seasoning. Divide among 6 small ramekin dishes.

to freeze Wrap ramekin dishes completely in foil, or make a foil 'lid' before labelling and freezing.

to thaw Thaw at room temperature for about 6 hours before serving.

Sardine Pâté

Ideal as a first course or as a sandwich filling (protein-rich for children's packed lunches).

**serves 6-8
as a first
course**

2 x 4¼ oz (120g) cans sardines in oil, well drained
4 oz (100g) butter, melted
juice of 1 lemon
salt
freshly ground black pepper

sauce
1 oz (25g) butter
1 oz (25g) flour
¼ pint (150ml) milk

First prepare the sauce by melting the butter in a pan. Stir in the flour and cook for 1 minute, then gradually blend in the milk and bring to the boil, stirring until thickened. Remove from the heat and allow to cool slightly then turn into a processor or blender. Add remaining ingredients and process for a few seconds until smooth and well blended. Taste and check seasoning then spoon into a small 1 pint (600 ml) terrine, level the top and chill in the refrigerator until set.

to freeze Freeze pâté in terrine, covered with foil, sealed and labelled.

to thaw Thaw in the refrigerator overnight, and serve as a first course with hot granary toast and butter.

Fine Brandied Liver Pâté

Perfect for a party, this pâté is simplicity itself to make, and freezes very well too.

makes 6 small individual pâtés

6 slices streaky bacon
1 lb (450g) chicken livers
8 oz (225g) butter, softened
4 tablespoons brandy
salt
ground black pepper

Heat the oven to 350°F/180°C/Gas 4. Line 6 ramekin dishes with the streaky bacon, pressing it firmly against the sides of the dish.

Put all the remaining ingredients in a processor or blender and process until smooth.

Pour this mixture into the dishes. Stand dishes in a roasting tin and carefully pour hot water around them to come half way up the sides. Cook in the oven for about 40 minutes until set. Allow to cool then chill in the refrigerator for about 6 hours before turning out of the dishes.

to freeze Wrap individually in foil. Seal, label and freeze.

to thaw Unwrap, thaw at room temperature for about 4 hours then serve, with hot toast and unsalted butter.

Rich Country Pâté

A rather special coarse pâté, which is nicest served with hot buttered toast.

serves 8

2 rashers streaky bacon
1 bayleaf
4 oz (100g) fresh white breadcrumbs
1 egg, beaten
⅛ pint (75 ml) port
4 oz (100g) belly pork, rind and bone removed
8 oz (225g) bacon pieces
8 oz (225g) pig's liver, sinews removed
8 oz (225g) chicken livers
1 fat clove garlic, crushed
½ teaspoon dried mixed herbs
½ teaspoon ground nutmeg
salt
freshly ground black pepper

Heat oven to 325°F/160°C/Gas 3. Well grease a 2 lb (900g) loaf tin. Remove the rind from the streaky bacon and flatten and stretch the rashers with the blade of a knife on a board. Put the bayleaf in the middle of the loaf tin and lay the bacon along the base of the tin.

Place all the remaining ingredients in a processor and process or, if using a blender, blend in small batches until well mixed. Don't over-process if you prefer a coarse pâté. Turn the mixture into the prepared tin. Cover with foil and put in a bain-marie or roasting tin half filled with hot water, and cook in the oven for about 2 hours. Clear juices should run from the pâté when pierced with a skewer.

to freeze

Cool completely, then turn out and wrap well with foil. Put in a polythene bag, seal and label, then freeze.

to thaw

Thaw at room temperature for about 6 hours before serving.

Unusual Dips

These dips should be served with potato crisps, sticks of celery, green pepper or carrot, cauliflower florets, as well as whole raw button mushrooms. Try making the Oriental one with your own home-made chutney.

Oriental Cheese Dip

serves 6

4 tablespoons mango chutney, chopped
8 oz (225g) cream cheese
a good pinch dry mustard
1 teaspoon curry powder

Put all the ingredients in a bowl and mix well until thoroughly blended.

Avocado and Onion Dip

serves 6

2 ripe avocado pears
3 oz (75g) cream cheese
juice of ½ lemon
1 oz (25g) onion, grated
freshly ground black pepper

Cut the pears in half and discard the stone. Scoop the flesh out into a bowl then mash with a silver fork. Add the remaining ingredients quickly, to prevent the avocado flesh becoming discoloured—and mix well until thoroughly blended. Use or freeze as soon as possible, as the avocado will begin to discolour.

to freeze   Place both dips in small, separate rigid containers, cover, seal, label and freeze.

to thaw   Thaw both at room temperature for about 5-6 hours then turn into glass serving dishes and serve with fresh crisp pieces of vegetables.

Cheese Mouthfuls

Good to go with drinks before dinner or to serve as one of the savouries for a drinks party.

makes about 65

8 oz (225g) well flavoured Cheddar cheese, grated
4 oz (100g) Danish blue cheese, crumbled
8 oz (225g) rich cream cheese
1 medium sized onion, finely grated
1 teaspoon Dijon mustard
about 3 teaspoons from the top of the milk
6 oz (175g) chopped walnuts

Put all the ingredients except the walnuts in a bowl and mix well until bound together. Form into small balls then roll balls in chopped walnuts until coated. Chill for about 8 hours in the refrigerator first, if serving straight away.

to freeze Open freeze on a tray, then pack in a polythene bag, seal, label, and return to the freezer.

to thaw Thaw in the refrigerator overnight. Spear each with a cocktail stick to serve.

Small Bacon and Onion Flans

Make in individual Yorkshire pudding tins. Serve warm as a first course or take them on picnics.

makes 20
small flans

8 oz (225g) plain flour
2 oz (50g) butter
2 oz (50g) lard
about 2 tablespoons water

filling
4 oz (100g) bacon pieces, finely chopped
1 medium sized onion, finely chopped
3 oz (75g) well flavoured Cheddar cheese, grated
2 eggs
6 tablespoons top of milk
2 teaspoons snipped chives
salt
freshly ground black pepper

Heat oven to 375°F/190°C/Gas 5. First make the pastry. Put flour in a bowl and rub in fats until mixture resembles fine breadcrumbs. Bind together with water to form a firm dough. Roll out on a floured surface and cut out into 20 circles large enough to line deep patty tins. Press the circles into the tins, line them with greaseproof paper and dried beans, and bake in the oven for about 15 minutes. Remove paper and beans.

Put the bacon in a non-stick pan and cook gently until the fat begins to run, then increase heat, add onion, and cook for about 5 minutes. Divide the mixture between the pastry cases, and sprinkle a little cheese in each. Blend together the eggs, milk, chives and seasoning, and spoon the mixture into the pastry cases.

Bake in the oven at 325°F/160°C/Gas 3 for about 20 minutes or until the filling has set. Remove from tins.

to freeze

Cool and open freeze, then stack on top of each other, interleaved with greaseproof paper. Pack in polythene bags, seal well, label and return to freezer.

to thaw

Heat from frozen at 350°F/180°C/Gas 4 for about 30 minutes until warmed through. Serve hot.

THE MAIN COURSE

When I am cooking a main course that I know freezes well, I
usually double up on the recipe and make one for supper that
night, and one for the freezer, usually with a special day in mind.
Perhaps the following week I will have a couple of very hectic
days with little or no time for cooking. I then label the dish with
the usual details—what it is, how many it is for, how long to cook
it and, in big letters, that it is for Thursday supper on the 8th
May or whenever. I also put it at the front of the freezer so that
I will see it! I find it best to keep most cooked dishes in the
freezer no longer than 3 months so they retain the very best
flavour. It is far better to turn the food over than be like a
squirrel with her nuts!

Fresh Fish Chowder

Serve with sliced toasted French bread topped with grated cheese and browned under a grill. Freeze the sauce only for use with freshly bought fish; a delicious and nutritious meal in moments!

serves 6

2 oz (50g) butter
2 medium sized onions, sliced
1 fat clove garlic, crushed
2 leeks, cut into rings
1 level tablespoon tomato purée
2 potatoes, diced
14 oz (397g) can tomatoes
1 pint (600ml) chicken stock
1 tablespoon freshly chopped parsley
1 teaspoon caster sugar
salt
freshly ground black pepper

for serving only
1 lb (450g) monk fish, skinned, boned and cut into bite-sized pieces
4 oz (100g) peeled prawns

Melt butter in a large pan, fry onions, garlic and leeks for about 5 minutes until tender. Add tomato purée, potato, tomatoes, stock, parsley, sugar and seasoning, and simmer for about 20 minutes until the potato is cooked.

to serve now
Put fish and prawns on top of sauce and simmer for a further 5 minutes until fish is cooked.

to freeze
Pour sauce into a rigid container, cool, cover, seal, label and freeze.

to thaw
Thaw at room temperature for about 6 hours then reheat in the oven at 375°F/190°C/Gas 5 for about 25 minutes until sauce is hot and bubbling. Put fish and prawns on top for last 5 minutes.

Broccoli and Haddock Mornay

Good idea to make when broccoli or calabrese is plentiful.

serves 4

1 lb (450g) fresh broccoli
1 lb (450g) haddock fillets, skinned
juice of ½ lemon
salt
freshly ground black pepper
generous 1 oz (25g) butter
1 oz (25g) flour
½ pint (300ml) milk
a little Dijon mustard
a little grated nutmeg
3 oz (75g) well flavoured Cheddar cheese

Divide each broccoli head into about four or eight pieces, according to size. Plunge into boiling salted water for 1 minute, drain and refresh with running cold water. Butter a shallow 2 pint (1.2 litre) ovenproof dish well, and place broccoli across the base. Cut haddock into 8 pieces and arrange on top of the broccoli. Sprinkle with lemon juice and seasoning.

Make a white sauce by melting the butter in a pan. Stir in flour and cook for 1 minute then gradually blend in the milk. Bring to the boil, stirring continuously, then when thickened, remove from heat and stir in mustard, nutmeg, a little seasoning and 1 oz (25g) of the cheese. Pour over the fish and sprinkle with remaining cheese.

to serve now

Heat oven to 425°F/220°C/Gas 7, and cook for about 25 minutes until brown and bubbling.

to freeze

Freeze without baking, covered with foil, sealed and labelled.

to thaw

Cook straight from frozen. Remove covering and bake at 400°F/200°C/ Gas 6 for about 55 minutes. Brown under a hot grill if liked.

Smoked Haddock Tagliatelle

Rather like kedgeree, but with noodles instead of rice.

serves 6

1 lb (450g) smoked haddock fillets
1 pint (600ml) milk
2 oz (50g) butter
8 oz (225g) onion, chopped
1 oz (25g) flour
salt
freshly ground black pepper
8 oz (225g) ribbon noodles
2 oz (50g) well flavoured Cheddar cheese, grated

Put the fish in a pan and add just enough milk to cover. Cook gently for about 5 minutes then remove from heat. Lift fish out with a slotted spoon, saving the milk for the sauce. Remove skin and bones from fish and flake flesh with a fork.

Melt butter in a pan, fry onion until soft, stir in flour and cook for a minute then blend in all the flavoured milk. Bring to the boil, stirring continuously, to make a thin sauce. Add seasoning and fish, then remove from the heat.

Cook the noodles in boiling salted water until just tender then drain and add to the fish sauce. Pour into a 3 pint (1.7 litre) ovenproof dish, and sprinkle grated cheese on top.

to serve now

Heat oven to 350°F/180°C/Gas 4, and bake for about 45 minutes until cheese is bubbling and a golden brown.

to freeze

Freeze without baking, wrapped in foil, sealed and labelled.

to thaw

Thaw at room temperature for about 8 hours then reheat in oven as above.

Crab and Fish Pie

Quick and easy to make, as a can of condensed soup is used for the sauce.

serves 6

1 lb (450g) cod
¼ pint (150ml) white wine
1 small onion, finely chopped
10 oz (295g) can condensed crab soup
4 oz (100g) crab meat
4 oz (100g) frozen peeled prawns, thawed
1 tablespoon freshly chopped parsley
salt
freshly ground black pepper
1 ½ lb (675g) potatoes
1 oz (25g) butter
milk

for serving only
lemon wedges

Put the cod in a pan with the wine and onion. Cover and poach for about 10 minutes until the fish is cooked. Lift the fish out of the pan and remove the skin and bones. Blend the soup with the cooking juices and onion in the pan and simmer for 2 minutes. Add the fish, crab, prawns, parsley and seasoning and bring to the boil, stirring. Cool.

Cook the potatoes in boiling salted water for about 20 minutes until tender. Drain and mash, then beat in butter and enough milk to make a smooth consistency. Season to taste. Pipe the potato through a large fluted nozzle around the edge of an 8 inch (20cm) shallow oval dish. Spoon the fish mixture into the centre and cool completely.

to freeze

Open freeze in dish until the pie is firm, then wrap completely in cling film, or cover with a foil lid, label and return to the freezer.

to thaw

Thaw at room temperature for about 6 hours. Remove lid and reheat at 425°F/220°C/Gas 7 for about 30 minutes until the potato is a pale golden brown and the fish mixture is piping hot. Garnish with lemon wedges.

Russian Fish Pie

This is fish in a creamy sauce encased in pastry. With both fish sauce and pastry stored in the freezer, you have the basics of a delicious and easy meal.

serves 4

12 oz (350g) cod fillet
½ pint (300ml) milk
1 oz (25g) butter
1 oz (25g) flour
1 tablespoon freshly chopped parsley
salt
freshly ground black pepper
juice of ½ lemon
2 hard-boiled eggs, roughly chopped

for serving only
14 oz (397g) packet frozen puff pastry, thawed
beaten egg to glaze

Poach the fish in the milk for about 10 minutes until the flesh will flake easily. Lift fish out of pan, remove and discard the dark skin and bones, and flake the flesh. Save the milk for the sauce.

Melt the butter in a pan, stir in the flour and cook for 2 minutes. Add the fishy milk and bring to the boil, stirring until thickened. Add the parsley, seasoning and lemon juice and mix well. Remove the sauce from the heat and then stir in the eggs and flaked fish. Leave to become quite cold.

to serve now

Roll out the pastry on a floured table to a 13 inch (32.5cm) square and trim the edges. Place the filling in the centre and brush the edges with beaten egg, then bring up the four corners of the pastry to the centre to form an envelope and seal the edges firmly. Place on a baking tray and brush with beaten egg. Cook in the oven at 425°F/220°C/Gas 7 for about 25 minutes until well risen and golden brown.

to freeze

Freeze filling separately in a rigid container, covered, sealed and labelled.

to thaw

Unwrap and thaw at room temperature for about 8 hours, then assemble and cook as suggested in the recipe.

RIGHT: *Cream of Mushroom Soup (page 31)*

Cod Catalan

A deliciously light dish, ideal for lunch.

serves 2

1 oz (25g) butter
1 large onion, sliced
1 clove garlic, crushed
1 oz (25g) flour
1 x 14 oz (397g) can tomatoes
1 tablespoon tomato purée

for serving only
2 oz (50g) stuffed olives, cut in half
2 x 6oz (175g) cod steaks
juice of ½ lemon
salt
freshly ground black pepper
1 oz (25g) hazelnuts, chopped
1 tablespoon freshly chopped parsley

Heat the butter in a pan and fry the onion for about 5 minutes until beginning to soften, then add the garlic. Sprinkle on the flour and blend in the tomatoes and purée. Bring to the boil, stirring continuously and cook for 2 minutes.

to serve now

Pour the sauce into a 2 pint (1.2 litre) ovenproof dish, and stir in the olives. Sprinkle the cod steaks with lemon juice and season well. Lay on top of the tomato sauce. Cover with a lid or piece of foil and bake in the oven at 375°F/190°C/Gas 5 for about 15 minutes until the fish is cooked. Just before serving sprinkle with the nuts and parsley.

to freeze

Freeze the sauce and fish separately. Pack sauce in a lidded plastic container and label. Wrap the cod steaks and label.

to thaw

Thaw at room temperature for about 4 hours then assemble and cook as recipe.

LEFT: *Cod Catalan (above)*

Beef and Red Bean Casserole

The kidney beans stretch the meat and it is a good dish for an inexpensive buffet supper.

serves 6

1 oz (25g) flour
salt
freshly ground black pepper
1 level teaspoon ground ginger
2 lb (900g) chuck steak, cubed
2 tablespoons sunflower oil

sauce
¼ teaspoon Tabasco sauce
8 oz (225g) can tomatoes
2 level tablespoons light muscovado sugar
2 tablespoons white wine vinegar
2 cloves garlic, crushed
1 bayleaf
1 red pepper, seeded and sliced
15¼ oz (432g) can red kidney beans, drained
4 oz (100g) button mushrooms, sliced

Heat the oven to 325°F/160°C/Gas 3.

Put the flour, salt, pepper and ginger into a polythene bag, add the meat and shake well until the meat is coated with the flour. Heat the oil in a large pan, add the meat and fry quickly until browned all over. Lift out and put into a 3 pint (1.7 litre) casserole dish.

In a bowl mix all the ingredients for the sauce—except the red pepper, kidney beans and mushrooms—then pour over the meat. Cover the casserole with a lid or piece of foil and cook in the oven for about 2 hours. Now add the red pepper, beans and mushrooms, and return to the oven for a further 30 minutes until the meat is tender. Remove the bayleaf, taste and check seasoning.

to freeze

Freeze in a rigid container in the usual way, or in the casserole dish then turn out and wrap in a double thickness of foil before returning to the freezer.

to thaw

Thaw for about 8 hours at room temperature then reheat thoroughly before serving with plain boiled rice and a green salad.

Braised Beef with Orange

There is a good amount of sauce with this so serve with plain boiled potatoes to mop it up.

serves 4-6

2 oz (50 g) flour
salt
freshly ground black pepper
1½ lb (675g) chuck steak, cubed
2 tablespoons sunflower oil
2 medium sized onions, chopped
8 oz (225g) carrots, peeled and sliced
6 sticks celery, chopped
1 pint (600ml) beef stock
1 sprig parsley
1 sprig thyme
2 bayleaves
1 small orange, quartered and pips removed
1 level tablespoon redcurrant jelly
8 oz (225g) mushrooms, sliced

Put the flour, salt and pepper in a polythene bag then add the meat and shake well so that the meat is evenly coated. Heat the oil in a large pan and fry the meat for about 10 minutes until browned all over. Lift out on to a plate with a slotted spoon.

Add the onions, carrots and celery to the fat left in the pan and fry for about 5 minutes until just beginning to soften, then add any flour left from coating the meat. Gradually stir in the stock, then add the meat, herbs, orange, and redcurrant jelly. Bring to the boil, cover and simmer gently for 2 hours then add mushrooms and cook for about another 30 minutes until the meat is tender. Remove the orange quarters and herbs before serving.

to freeze

Pour into a rigid container, cool, seal, label and freeze.

to thaw

Thaw at room temperature for about 8 hours then reheat until piping hot.

St Edward's Beef

A sound and hearty casserole, which needs only the smallest amount of attention.

serves 6

2 lb (900g) stewing steak, cubed
1½ oz (40g) flour
2-3 tablespoons sunflower oil
salt
freshly ground black pepper
8 oz (225g) onions, sliced
2 fat cloves garlic, crushed
4 oz (100g) mushrooms, sliced
1 red pepper, seeded and sliced
2 tablespoons blackcurrant jelly
¼ pint (150ml) inexpensive port
¾ pint (450 ml) good beef stock

Put the meat in a polythene bag with flour and shake until well coated. Heat oil in a pan and fry meat for about 10 minutes until browned. Stir in all remaining ingredients, including any flour left in the bag, bring to the boil, cover and simmer gently for about 2½ hours until the meat is tender. Stir occasionally, and taste for seasoning.

to freeze Turn into a rigid container, cool, cover, label and freeze.

to thaw Thaw at room temperature for about 8 hours. Heat oven to 375°F/190°C/Gas 5. Turn casserole into an ovenproof dish, cover with a lid and reheat for about 40 minutes until piping hot. Serve with a green salad and crusty French bread.

Speciality Beef

A good stew for a more special occasion. Serve with buttery mashed potatoes to soak up the sauce.

serves 4-6
1½ lb (675g) good stewing steak
6 oz (175g) streaky bacon, cut into strips
1 oz (25g) flour
½ pint (300ml) good beef stock
¼ pint (150ml) red wine
1 bayleaf
½ teaspoon freshly chopped mixed herbs
salt
freshly ground black pepper
4 oz (100g) small onions, peeled

Heat the oven to 325°F/160°C/Gas 3.

Cut the steak into 1½ inch (3.5-4 cm) cubes. Put the bacon in a nonstick pan and heat gently until fat begins to run, then increase heat and fry quickly for about 5 minutes until beginning to brown. Lift bacon into a 3 pint (1.7 litre) ovenproof casserole dish and then fry the steak in the fat remaining in the pan until brown all over. Remove to casserole.

Stir flour into fat and cook for 2 minutes, then gradually blend in the stock and wine. Bring to the boil, stirring. Once thickened add the bayleaf, herbs and seasoning. Pour this over the bacon and meat, cover the casserole and cook in the oven for about 1½ hours. Then add the onions and cook for about another hour or until the meat is really tender. Taste and check seasoning before serving.

to freeze
Cool then turn into a rigid container, cover, seal, label and freeze.

to thaw
Thaw at room temperature for about 10 hours then reheat in the oven at 325°F/160°C/Gas 3 for about 40 minutes until piping hot.

Beef of the Mountains

Slices of braising beef in a herb and tomato sauce, delicious with buttery boiled potatoes.

serves 6

2 tablespoons sunflower oil
6 slices braising beef, about 6 oz (175g) each
3 medium onions, sliced
1 oz (25g) flour
14 oz (397g) can tomatoes
1 tablespoon freshly chopped mixed herbs
salt
freshly ground black pepper

Heat the oil in a pan, add the beef and fry quickly to brown all over. Lift out and put on one side. Add the onions to the fat left in the pan and fry quickly for about 5 minutes until pale golden brown. Stir in the flour and cook for a minute before adding the tomatoes, herbs and seasoning.

Lay the beef on top of vegetable mixture, cover with a tight fitting lid, and simmer very gently for about 2½ hours or until the meat is tender. Taste and check seasoning before serving.

to freeze Pack in a polythene container, cover, seal, label and freeze.

to thaw Thaw at room temperature for about 7 hours then reheat in the oven at 375°F/190°C/Gas 5 for about 35 minutes until heated through.

Highland Beef with Herbed Dumplings

This should ideally be frozen in the serving container so that the dumplings are not handled too much.

serves 4

1 lb (450g) stewing steak, cubed
1 oz (25g) seasoned flour
1 tablespoon sunflower oil
1 large onion, sliced
¾ pint (450ml) good beef stock
2 good tablespoons tomato purée
1 tablespoon freshly chopped mixed herbs
salt
freshly ground black pepper

dumplings
4 oz (100g) self-raising, flour
1 teaspoon salt
2 oz (50g) shredded suet
2 tablespoons freshly chopped parsley
about 4 tablespoons cold water

Heat the oven to 325°F/160°C/Gas 3.

Toss meat in seasoned flour. Heat oil in a large pan, add onion and cook for about 5 minutes until golden brown. Add meat and any seasoned flour left and fry quickly until browned all over, then gradually blend in stock, purée and herbs. Bring to the boil, stirring all the time, then turn into a 2 pint (1.2 litre) casserole dish. Season, cover with a lid and cook in the oven for about 2 hours until the meat is tender.

Mix all the ingredients for the dumplings and shape into 8 small balls. The mixture should be a soft dough and not too sticky to handle. Add to the casserole for the last 25-35 minutes of cooking time.

to freeze   Cool then wrap well with foil, seal, label and freeze.

to thaw   Thaw at room temperature for about 8 hours then reheat in the oven at 350°F/180°C/Gas 4 for about 45 minutes until heated through.

Mortimer Beef

A delicious fruity casserole best served with boiled rice and a green salad

serves 8

2 tablespoons sunflower oil
2½ lb (1.1kg) chuck steak, cubed
8 oz (225g) onion, chopped
2 oz (50g) flour
1 pint (600ml) cider
½ pint (300ml) beef stock
4 oz (100g) dried apricot pieces
2 oranges, quartered and pips removed
2 tablespoons vinegar
1 level teaspoon curry powder
1 tablespoon soy sauce
2 cloves garlic, crushed
4 oz (100g) seedless raisins
1 oz (25g) dark muscovado sugar
1 sprig thyme
salt
freshly ground black pepper

Heat the oven to 325°F/160°C/Gas 3.

Heat the oil in a large pan and fry the meat until browned all over. Lift out and put into a 4 pint (2.2 litre) casserole dish. Add the onions to the oil remaining in the pan and fry until lightly browned. Stir in the flour and cook for 1 minute, then blend in the cider and stock. Add the remaining ingredients, and bring to the boil, stirring continuously. Pour over the meat, cover the casserole with a lid or piece of foil and cook in the oven for about 3 hours until the meat is tender. Taste and check the seasoning, and discard the thyme and pieces of orange.

to freeze Turn into a rigid container, cool, cover, label and freeze.

to thaw Thaw at room temperature for about 12 hours, then reheat gently in a saucepan until piping hot. Sprinkle with some chopped parsley just before serving.

Bombay Curry

This is a mild curry; if you like it stronger add more curry powder. Serve with sambals and side dishes of sliced tomato, sliced banana, mixed shelled nuts and chopped mild onion.

serves 4

2 tablespoons sunflower oil
1 large onion, chopped
about 2 level tablespoons curry powder
1 oz (25g) flour
8 oz (227g) can tomatoes
1 good tablespoon tomato purée
½ pint (300ml) beef stock
1 lb (450g) good quality stewing beef, cubed
1 small cooking apple, peeled, cored and chopped
2 oz (50g) sultanas
salt
freshly ground black pepper

Heat oil in a large pan and fry onion for about 5 minutes until golden brown. Stir in curry powder and flour, then blend in tomatoes and purée with the stock. Cook over a medium heat, stirring, until oil starts to come through, then add meat. Cover with a lid, bring to the boil and simmer for about 2½ hours until the meat is tender. Add the apple and sultanas and season to taste half an hour before the end of cooking.

to freeze

Allow to cool then pour into a rigid container, seal, label and freeze.

to thaw

Thaw at room temperature for about 6 hours, then reheat gently in a pan until piping hot.

Curry Cottage Pie

This is a slightly more exotic version of the family favourite.

serves 8

2 tablespoons sunflower oil
8 oz (225g) onion, chopped
2 good tablespoons tomato purée
salt
freshly ground black pepper
1 oz (25g) flour
1 pint (600ml) good beef stock
2 lb (900g) raw lean minced beef
2 teaspoons curry powder
2 tablespoons mango chutney
1 oz (25g) sultanas
8 oz (225g) carrots, grated
1 tablespoon finely chopped parsley
2 lb (900g) potatoes, boiled and mashed with a knob of butter and a little milk

Heat oil in a large pan, add onion and fry gently for about 5 minutes until soft and lightly coloured. Stir in the tomato purée, seasoning and flour, and cook for about 2 minutes. Blend in stock with the mince, curry powder, chutney and sultanas and bring to the boil, stirring. Cover with a lid and simmer gently for about an hour until the meat is tender, then stir in carrots and parsley. Bring back to the boil, simmer for 2 minutes then leave to cool.

Turn mince into a 3 pint (1.7 litre) pie dish. Spoon or pipe potatoes over the top of the mince.

to freeze   Open freeze, then wrap in foil, label and return to freezer.

to thaw   Thaw overnight at room temperature, remove wrapping and cook in oven at 400°F/200°C/Gas 6 for about 45 minutes. Garnish with some freshly chopped parsley before serving.

Spiced Stuffed Peppers

This is a delicious way of serving home-grown green peppers.

serves 4

2 onions, *chopped*
1 clove garlic, *crushed*
12 oz (350g) *raw minced beef*
2 oz (50g) *flour*
½ pint (300ml) *water*
1 teaspoon Worcestershire sauce
1 beef stock cube
salt and freshly ground black pepper
2 large green peppers

sauce
1 oz (25g) butter
1 oz (25g) flour
½ pint (300ml) milk
2 oz (50g) well flavoured Cheddar cheese, grated
1 teaspoon Dijon mustard
salt and freshly ground black pepper

Put the onion, garlic and mince in a non-stick pan and fry gently to brown for about 5 minutes. Stir in the flour and water, Worcestershire sauce and add the crumbled stock cube and seasoning. Cover and simmer gently for about 30 minutes until tender, then adjust seasoning.

Cut the peppers in half and remove the seeds and any 'pith'. Cook the pepper shells in boiling water for about 5 minutes, drain well on kitchen paper, and place in an ovenproof dish so that they just touch. Fill with the beef mixture.

For the sauce, melt the butter in a pan and stir in the flour. Cook for 1 minute, add the milk and bring to the boil, stirring. Simmer until thickened then remove from the heat and stir in the cheese, mustard and seasoning. Spoon sauce over the peppers in the dish.

to serve now Heat the oven to 350°F/180°C/Gas 4. Bake peppers, uncovered, for about 30 minutes until piping hot.

to freeze Pack in a rigid container, seal, label and freeze uncooked.

to thaw Thaw at room temperature for about 8 hours, then cook as above.

American Meatballs

A delicious way of eating minced beef, and it's particularly popular with the children.

serves 8

2 lb (900g) minced beef
1 large onion, finely chopped
1 fat clove garlic, crushed
2 eggs, beaten
2 oz (50g) fresh white breadcrumbs
½ teaspoon dried mixed herbs
salt
freshly ground black pepper
2 tablespoons sunflower oil for frying

sauce
8 oz (225g) mushrooms, sliced
1 oz (25g) flour
1 pint (600 ml) good stock
4 level tablespoons tomato purée
4 oz (100g) red kidney beans, soaked overnight
salt and freshly ground black pepper

Heat the oven to 325°F/160°C/Gas 3.

In a bowl mix all the ingredients for the meatballs until smooth, and then, with floured hands, form mixture into 24 small balls. Heat oil in a pan and fry meatballs quickly until browned all over. Lift them into a 3 pint (1.7 litre) casserole with a slotted spoon.

For the sauce, fry the mushrooms in the fat left in the pan for about 3 minutes, stir in the flour and cook for a few moments then blend in the stock and tomato purée. Bring to the boil, stirring continually. Stir in the beans and seasoning and simmer for about 15 minutes then pour sauce over meatballs, cover casserole with a lid and cook in the oven for about an hour until the meat is tender.

to freeze

Allow to cool then turn into a rigid container, cover, seal, label and freeze.

to thaw

Thaw at room temperature for about 8 hours, then reheat in the oven at 350°F/180°C/Gas 4 for about 45 minutes until hot and bubbling. Serve with boiled rice.

Steak, Kidney and Mushroom Pie

A great standby for the freezer. I often make a couple of these at a time—one for now, then one which I freeze for later in the month.

serves 4

1 lb (450g) skirt beef, cubed
4 oz (100g) beef kidney, core removed and cubed
1 oz (25g) flour
1 oz (25g) dripping
4 oz (100g) mushrooms, sliced
1 large onion, chopped
½ pint (300ml) good beef stock
salt
freshly ground black pepper
8 oz (227g) packet frozen puff pastry, thawed
a little milk to glaze

Toss meats in seasoned flour. Melt dripping, add meat, mushrooms and onion, and fry quickly until meat is browned. Blend in the stock and bring to the boil, stirring. Add seasoning, cover pan with a lid and simmer gently for about 2 hours until the meat is tender. Taste and check seasoning.

Put a pie funnel in a 1 pint (600ml) pie dish, spoon the meat around it and chill. Heat the oven to 425°F/220°C/Gas 7.

Roll out pastry on a lightly floured surface and use to cover the pie. Seal and crimp the edges, make a slit in the centre to let the steam escape and use any trimmings to decorate the top.

to serve now

Heat oven to 425°F/220°C/Gas 7. Glaze the pastry, and cook in the oven for 30-35 minutes until well risen and golden brown, and the meat has heated through.

to freeze

Freeze pie without cooking, wrapped in foil, sealed, and labelled.

to thaw

Thaw at room temperature for about 6 hours, then cook as above.

Creamy Veal

Stewing veal is sometimes difficult to get, so you could use casserole turkey which is often available in freezer centres. This is very simple to make, but it needs really slow cooking, either on the top of the hob or in the oven.

serves 4

1 lb (450g) stewing veal, cubed
2 medium sized onions, quartered
2 large carrots, cut into 8 pieces
1 bayleaf
1 sprig of parsley
salt
freshly ground black pepper
¼ pint (150ml) white wine or cider
¼ pint (150ml) light veal or chicken stock
1 oz (25g) butter
1 oz (25g) flour

for serving only
5oz (150g) carton single cream

Put all the ingredients, except the butter, flour and cream, in a pan and bring to the boil. Simmer gently for about 1½ hours until the meat is tender. Lift meat and vegetables on to a serving dish with a slotted spoon and keep warm. Remove and discard the herbs.

Melt the butter in a pan, stir in the flour and cook for 2 minutes then gradually blend in the cooking liquid. Bring to the boil, stirring all the time.

to serve now
Once sauce is thickened, stir in the cream, taste and check seasoning. Heat gently until it just reaches boiling point then pour sauce over meat and vegetables. Serve.

to freeze
Freeze sauce, meat and vegetables together (before adding cream) in a covered and labelled container.

to thaw
Thaw at room temperature for about 6 hours then stir cream into the sauce and reheat in the oven at 350°F/180°C/Gas 4 for about 40 minutes until heated through.

Italian Veal

A delicious, less usual casserole which goes especially well with rice.

serves 4

1 tablespoon sunflower oil
1 oz (25g) butter
1½lb (675g) casserole veal
1 large onion, chopped
1 fat clove garlic, crushed
1 oz (25g) flour
¼ pint (150ml) cider
¼ pint (150ml) chicken stock
14 oz (397g) can tomatoes
salt
freshly ground black pepper
4 oz (100g) button mushrooms, sliced
a little chopped parsley to garnish

Heat the oil and butter in a pan and fry the veal, onion and garlic for about 5 minutes. Stir in the flour and cook for a minute. Blend in the cider and stock and bring to the boil. Add the tomatoes and season well.

Cover the pan and simmer for about 1½ hours or until the veal is tender. Add the mushrooms for the last half hour of cooking time. Taste and check seasoning.

to freeze

Cool then pack in a rigid container, cover, seal, label and freeze.

to thaw

Thaw at room temperature for about 8 hours then reheat at 400°F/ 200°C/Gas 6 in a covered ovenproof casserole dish for about 25 minutes until piping hot. Garnish with chopped parsley.

Hampstead Pork

This is a good dish for entertaining. Serve it with boiled rice and a green salad.

serves 6

2 oz (50g) butter
1½ lb (675g) pork fillet, cubed
12 oz (350g) onions, chopped
1 oz (25g) flour
½ pint (300ml) good stock
½ pint (300ml) dry cider
thinly peeled rind of 1 lemon, in large pieces
6 oz (175g) button mushrooms, sliced,
1 level teaspoon paprika pepper
salt
freshly ground black pepper

for serving only
5 oz (150g) carton soured cream
freshly chopped parsley to garnish

Heat the oven to 325°F/160°C/Gas 3.

Melt the butter in a pan and quickly fry the meat until browned all over then lift out with a slotted spoon into a 3 pint (1.7 litre) casserole. Fry onions in fat left in the pan for about 5 minutes until golden brown. Stir in flour and gradually blend in stock and cider, stirring until thickened. Stir in the lemon rind, mushrooms, paprika, and seasoning. Pour sauce over the meat, cover casserole with a lid and cook in the oven for about 40 minutes until the meat is tender.

Remove the lemon rind and discard, taste and check seasoning.

to freeze

Freeze before adding cream and parsley. Turn into a rigid container, cover, seal, label then freeze.

to thaw

Thaw at room temperature for about 8 hours. Reheat in a covered casserole at 350°F/180°C/Gas 4 for about 30 minutes until piping hot. Stir in cream and sprinkle with parsley before serving.

Somerset Pork

Pork in a creamy sauce with apple and onion. I'm not a great one for piped potato but this does look pretty around the dish.

serves 6

1 oz (25g) butter
1 tablespoon sunflower oil
1½ lb (675g) pork fillet, cut into ½ inch (1-1.5cm) slices
1 large onion, chopped
1 Bramley apple, chopped
1 oz (25g) flour
½ pint (300ml) milk
½ pint (300ml) water
1 chicken stock cube
salt and freshly ground black pepper
1 lb (450g) potatoes, boiled and mashed with 1 egg yolk,
1 oz (25g) butter and the top off the milk

for serving only
fresh watercress

Heat butter and oil in a pan and quickly fry pork until browned all over. Lift out with a slotted spoon and put to one side. Add onion to fat left in pan and fry for about 10 minutes until golden brown, then add apple and flour. Cook for 1 minute then gradually blend in milk, water and stock cube. Bring to the boil, stirring, and once thickened add seasoning. Return pork to the pan, bring to the boil in the sauce and simmer for about 10 minutes until pork cooks through.

Pipe the mashed potato around the edge of a shallow dish with a star shaped nozzle.

to serve now

Brown potato piping on dish under a hot grill, then pour hot pork into the centre of the dish. Garnish with watercress and serve.

to freeze

Freeze pork and potato piping in dish without browning the potato.

to thaw

Thaw for about 8 hours at room temperature. Put a piece of foil over the meat but leave the potato showing, and reheat in the oven at 400°F/200°C/Gas 6 for about 25 minutes until the potato has browned and the pork is hot. Remove foil, garnish with watercress and serve.

Norfolk Hotpot

This hotpot takes time to make but is so good. Should the bacon stock be on the salty side then use a stock cube and water instead in the sauce. A knuckle of forehock of bacon is one of the cheaper cuts.

serves 6

1 knuckle of forehock of bacon
1 bayleaf
1 lb (450g) onions, sliced
1 lb (450g) potatoes, peeled and sliced

sauce
2 oz (50g) butter
2 oz (50g) flour
¾ pint (450ml) milk
¾ pint (450ml) bacon stock
salt
freshly ground black pepper

Soak the knuckle in a pan of cold water overnight then throw away the water. Cover knuckle with fresh water, and add bayleaf. Put lid on pan, bring to the boil, and simmer gently for about 2 hours until tender. Lift knuckle out of stock and allow to cool. When cool, take meat off bone, and discard skin, fat and bones. Cut meat into small cubes.

Bring a large pan of salted water to the boil, add onions and potatoes and simmer for about 10 minutes. Drain and put about 15 of the largest slices of potato aside to cover the casserole.

To prepare the sauce, melt butter in a pan, stir in flour and cook for 1 minute. Gradually blend in milk and stock, and stir until thickened. Taste then add seasoning. Mix sauce with bacon, onion and potato, except for the reserved slices. Check seasoning then pour into a 3 pint (1.7 litre) casserole. Top with reserved slices of potato.

to freeze Wrap casserole with foil, seal, label and freeze for up to 3 weeks.

to thaw Thaw at room temperature for about 8 hours then cook, covered, in the oven at 375°F/190°C/Gas 5, for about an hour. Remove the lid for the last 30 minutes' cooking time.

American Beanpot

This dish is a favourite with teenagers, and it's also very quick to prepare as the meat is not fried first.

serves 4

1 lb (450g) lean casserole pork, cubed
1 medium onion, sliced
3 tablespoons tomato purée
1 oz (25g) flour
1 fat clove garlic, crushed
¾ pint (450 ml) good stock
salt
freshly ground black pepper
dash of Tabasco sauce
15¼ oz (432g) can red kidney beans, drained
4 oz (100g) mushrooms, sliced

Heat the oven to 325°F/160°C/Gas 3.

Put pork and onion in a 2 pint (1.2 litre) casserole. Blend the tomato purée and flour in a bowl, mix in all the remaining ingredients (except beans and mushrooms), and pour this over the meat. Cover casserole with a lid and cook in the oven for about 2 hours until the meat is tender.

Add beans and mushrooms half an hour before the end of cooking time.

to freeze Allow to cool then pour into a rigid container, seal, label and freeze.

to thaw Thaw at room temperature for about 8 hours, then reheat in a pan until piping hot. Check seasoning and serve.

Danish Frikadeller

These Danish meatballs are traditionally a flat oval shape. They go very well with spiced red cabbage (see following recipe).

makes 12

1 lb (450g) minced pork
1 medium sized onion, finely chopped
2oz (50g) white breadcrumbs
4 tablespoons milk
1 egg, beaten
salt
freshly ground black pepper

for serving only
2 tablespoons oil

Put all the ingredients except the oil into a bowl. Mix well and chill in the refrigerator for about 3 hours so that the mixture is easy to handle.

Divide the mixture into 12 equal portions and with floured hands shape them into balls then flatten them out to ovals.

to serve now
Heat the oil in a large frying pan and fry the frikadeller gently for about 15 minutes, until golden brown on both sides. Serve on a bed of spiced red cabbage.

to freeze
Pack raw into a polythene box and interleave with pieces of greaseproof paper so that they are easy to separate when frozen. Cover with a lid, label and freeze.

to thaw
Cook straight from frozen, but for about 30 minutes, and serve as suggested above.

Red Cabbage

Delicious served with Danish Frikadeller, but equally good with plain grilled pork chops.

serves 4

1 small red cabbage
12 oz (350g) cooking apples, sliced
¼ pint (150ml) water
1½ oz (40g) sugar
salt
3 cloves
5 tablespoons vinegar
2oz (50g) butter
1 tablespoon redcurrant jelly

Finely shred the cabbage and place with apples and water in a pan. Add sugar, salt and cloves, cover and simmer until tender (about 45 minutes)

to serve now
Remove the cloves, add the vinegar, butter and redcurrant jelly and stir until the butter has melted. Taste and adjust seasoning.

to freeze
Turn into a rigid container (not a foil one), cool, cover, label and freeze.

to thaw
Thaw overnight in the refrigerator, put in a non-stick pan and reheat gently, stirring.

Justin Pork Chops

An unusual and surprisingly simple way of preparing a supper dish. This recipe is easily adapted to serve any number of people.

serves 4

4 lean pork chops
Dijon mustard
about 4 oz (100g) light muscovado sugar
2 small oranges, segmented, with all pips and pith removed

Trim the chops of excess fat, then spread with mustard on both sides. Put sugar on a plate and roll chops in sugar until well coated. Lay in a greased shallow ovenproof dish. Arrange orange segments on top of chops and pour over any orange juice you will have collected when segmenting them.

to serve now
Heat the oven to 375°F/190°C/Gas 5. Bake uncovered for about 45 minutes until the chops are tender, basting occasionally.

to freeze
Best frozen raw with sugar and orange topping. Overwrap individually in foil, and then stack carefully in polythene bag.

to thaw
Thaw for about 6 hours at room temperature. Unwrap gently, and lift on to greased dish. Bake as in recipe.

Barbecued Spare Rib Chops

Spare rib chops are cheaper than loin chops and very good served this way. Trim off any excess fat before browning them.

serves 4

4 large or 8 small spare rib chops

sauce
1 rounded tablespoon apricot jam
1 teaspoon Dijon mustard
good pinch cayenne pepper
1 fat clove garlic, crushed
1 tablespoon Worcestershire sauce
3 tablespoons tomato ketchup
1 tablespoon soy sauce
salt
freshly ground black pepper

Put the chops in a non-stick pan and fry gently until fat begins to run, then increase heat and fry quickly for about 10 minutes until browned all over. Lift into a shallow ovenproof dish so that they just touch.

Mix together jam, mustard, cayenne pepper, garlic and Worcestershire sauce until blended then stir in remaining ingredients. Season and pour over the chops, coating them evenly. Cover with a piece of foil.

to serve now
Heat the oven to 350°F/180°C/Gas 4. Cook in the oven for about an hour until the meat is tender. Serve with rice and a green salad.

to freeze
Freeze without cooking in the oven, wrapped in foil, and then a polythene bag, sealed and labelled.

to thaw
Thaw in the refrigerator overnight then cook as suggested above.

Sweet and Sour Sausages

A popular dish for hungry teenagers, and it is best accompanied by French bread.

serves 4

1 scant tablespoon sunflower oil
8 thick pork sausages
1 onion, chopped
2 carrots, cut into long strips
1 leek, finely sliced
2 sticks celery, sliced
4 teaspoons cornflour
2 teaspoons sugar
½ pint (300ml) water
2 tablespoons tomato ketchup
1 tablespoon white wine vinegar
1 tablespoon soy sauce

Heat the oil in a pan and fry sausages until browned all over, then lift on to a plate. Add onion, carrot, leek and celery to the pan and fry gently until beginning to soften. Put cornflour and sugar in a bowl and gradually stir in the water. Add ketchup, vinegar and soy sauce, then pour into the pan and bring to the boil, stirring.

Once thickened return sausages to the pan and simmer with a lid for about 20 minutes until the vegetables are tender.

to freeze Turn into a rigid container, cool, cover, seal, label and freeze—for no longer than a month.

to thaw Thaw at room temperature for about 5 hours then heat oven to 400°F/200°C/Gas 6. Turn sausages into an ovenproof dish, cover with a lid, and reheat in the oven for about 30 minutes until heated through.

Family Sausage Roll

Quicker to make than a batch of small sausage rolls, and the cheese adds flavour to the pastry.

serves 4

filling
1 lb (450g) pork sausagemeat
4 oz (100g) fresh white breadcrumbs
1 egg
2 tablespoons freshly chopped parsley
salt
freshly ground black pepper

pastry
1 oz (25g) lard
1 oz (25g) margarine
4 oz (100g) plain flour
3 oz (75g) well flavoured Cheddar cheese, grated
generous tablespoon water to mix

for serving only
a little beaten egg to glaze

First prepare the filling. Mix together all the ingredients in a bowl until well blended, then stand it on one side.

To make the pastry, rub the fats into the flour until it resembles fine breadcrumbs, then stir in grated cheese and add sufficient water to mix to a firm dough. Roll out on a lightly floured surface to an oblong about 11 x 7 inches (27.5 x 17.5 cm) then lift on to a baking tray.

Arrange filling down centre of pastry to form a long sausage. Brush pastry borders with a little water, fold both long sides over filling so they overlap. Tuck the ends of pastry under the roll and decorate with pastryleaves.

to serve
now

Heat the oven to 425°F/220°C/Gas 7. Brush pastry with beaten egg and bake in the oven for about 40 minutes until golden.

to freeze

Freeze without cooking, wrapped in foil, sealed and labelled.

to thaw

Thaw at room temperature for about 8 hours, brush with beaten egg and bake as above.

Kidney Casserole with Parsley Dumplings

Delicious and inexpensive. Try to cook and freeze in the same container, so that the dumplings are handled as little as possible.

serves 4

1½ oz (40g) seasoned flour
4 pig kidneys, skinned, cored and sliced
3 tablespoons sunflower oil
1 large onion, chopped
2 oz (50g) mushrooms, sliced
¼ pint (150ml) good stock
¼ pint (150ml) left-over red wine (or more stock)
1 tablespoon redcurrant jelly

dumplings
4 oz (100g) self-raising flour
2 oz (50g) shredded suet
salt
1 tablespoon freshly chopped parsley
about 5 tablespoons water

Put the seasoned flour in a polythene bag, add kidneys and shake well until coated. Heat oil in a pan and sauté onion until beginning to soften then add kidneys and fry until colour changes. Add the mushrooms and any flour left from the bag, and cook for 1 minute. Blend in the stock, wine and the jelly and bring to the boil, stirring continuously. Remove from heat once thickened.

Mix the ingredients for the dumplings with enough water to give a soft but not sticky dough. Shape into 10 small balls and put on top of kidneys. Return to the heat. Cover and simmer for about 20 minutes until dumplings are cooked.

to freeze

Cool then spoon carefully into a rigid container (or freeze in cooking dish). Cover, seal, label and freeze.

to thaw

Thaw at room temperature for about 6 hours then reheat in oven until heated right through (about 40 minutes at 350°F/180°C/Gas 4).

Fillet of Lamb in Paprika Sauce

A delicious way of serving lamb, and it's so incredibly simple to prepare!

serves 4

2 oz (50g) butter
1 large onion, chopped
1 fat clove garlic, crushed
½ oz (15g) flour
14 oz (397g) can tomatoes
1 tablespoon tomato purée
1 tablespoon muscovado sugar
2 tablespoons paprika pepper
3 tablespoons cider vinegar
salt
freshly ground black pepper
1 lb (450g) lamb fillet, cubed

Heat the oven to 350°F/180°C/Gas 4.

Put the butter in a small pan and fry onion and garlic for about 5 minutes until golden brown. Stir in the flour and cook for 1 minute. Add tomatoes, purée, sugar, paprika and vinegar and cook together for about 4 minutes. Taste and adjust seasoning.

Arrange lamb in a shallow ovenproof dish and pour over the sauce. Cover and cook in the oven for about 45 minutes until the lamb is tender.

to freeze

Cool, cover, label and freeze.

to thaw

Thaw at room temperature for about 6 hours then reheat in the oven as outlined in recipe.

Welsh Lamb Casserole

Use fillet of lamb from the neck of lamb or you could use middle neck of lamb chops for this.

serves 6

1 oz (25g) butter
1½ lb (675g) fillet of lamb, cubed
8 oz (225g) carrots, peeled and sliced
8 oz (225g) leeks, washed and sliced
1½ oz (40g) flour
½ pint (300ml) cider
¼ pint (150ml) milk
about 1 teaspoon salt
freshly ground black pepper
1 bayleaf

Melt the butter in a large pan, and fry lamb for about 5 minutes until browned all over. Lift out on to a plate with a slotted spoon.

Fry the carrots and leeks in the fat left in the pan for about 5 minutes until beginning to soften, then stir in flour and cook for a couple of minutes. Gradually blend in the cider, then bring to the boil. When thickened, stir in the milk, add the seasoning and bayleaf, and bring back to the boil. Cover and simmer gently for about 2 hours until meat is tender. Remove the bayleaf before serving and, if necessary, thin down with a little extra milk.

to freeze Turn into a rigid container, allow to cool, seal, label and freeze.

to thaw Thaw at room temperature for about 8 hours. Reheat in a pan until piping hot.

Irish Stew

Good way of using neck when you have perhaps bought and frozen half a lamb. Although a true Irish stew has no carrots we prefer them added, and it's perfect for a cold wintry day.

serves 4

8 middle neck lamb chops
1 lb (450g) onions, sliced
2 lb (900g) potatoes, sliced
salt
freshly ground black pepper
8 oz (225g) carrots, sliced
water

Heat the oven to 325°F/160°C/Gas 3.

Trim any excess fat off lamb. Put half the onion into a 3 pint (1.7 litre) casserole, add half the potato and then the meat, seasoning each layer well. Cover with the carrots, then add the remaining onion and finish with a layer of potato. Add enough water to come half way up the casserole.

Cover and cook in the oven for about an hour, then remove the lid and cook for a further hour.

to freeze   Cool, turn into a rigid container cover, label and freeze.

to thaw   Thaw overnight in the refrigerator then reheat in the oven at 350°F/180°C/Gas 4 for about 45 minutes until heated through.

Lamb Burgers

Many butchers are now selling minced lamb, and these lamb burgers make a refreshing change from beefburgers.

makes 8

1 oz (25g) butter
1 small onion, finely chopped
12 oz (350g) raw minced lamb
3oz (75g) fresh white breadcrumbs
1 egg, beaten
salt
freshly ground black pepper

for serving only
oil for frying

Melt the butter in a pan and fry the onion until golden brown. Spoon onion into a mixing bowl and add remaining ingredients. Mix thoroughly until blended.

Divide the mixture into 8 equal sized pieces, and with lightly floured hands shape each into a burger. Chill well.

to serve now

Heat the oil in a pan and fry burgers gently for about 15 minutes until cooked right through. Turn once during cooking. Serve with onion or mint sauce. (For onion sauce, see opposite.)

to freeze

Freeze uncooked, interleaved with greaseproof paper, wrapped in foil, sealed and labelled.

to thaw

Cook straight from frozen as in recipe but increase cooking time to about 25 minutes.

Onion Sauce

Delicious accompaniment to the lamb burgers on the previous page.

2oz (50g) butter
8 oz (225g) onions, sliced
2 oz (50g) flour
1 pint (600ml) water
2 beef stock cubes
3 tablespoons tomato ketchup
a dash of Worcestershire sauce
¼ level teaspoon dried marjoram
salt
freshly ground black pepper

Melt the butter in a pan, add the onions and fry for about 10 minutes until golden brown. Stir in the flour and cook for 2 minutes. Add the water and crumbled stock cubes and bring to the boil, stirring until thickened. Add the tomato ketchup, Worcestershire sauce, marjoram, salt and pepper and stir well. Cover with a lid, reduce the heat and simmer gently for about 20 minutes.

to freeze Allow to cool, turn into a rigid container, seal, label and freeze.

to thaw Thaw at room temperature for about 4 hours, turn into a pan and reheat gently.

Lamb Beanfeast

This dish is really quick and easy to make. Put the beans to soak the night before.

serves 4-6

4 oz (100g) haricot beans, soaked overnight
3 rashers streaky bacon, chopped
1 large onion, chopped
2 lb (1 kg) neck of lamb chops
1 oz (25g) flour
14 oz (397g) can tomatoes
½ pint (300ml) good stock
1 teaspoon dried rosemary
salt
freshly ground black pepper

Heat oven to 350°F/180°C/Gas 4.

Put the bacon in a non-stick pan and heat gently until fat begins to run out. Then increase heat, add onion and fry for about 5 minutes until onion is golden brown. With a slotted spoon, lift the onion and bacon into a 2 pint (1.2 litre) ovenproof dish.

Fry the chops until browned on both sides in the juices left in the pan. Lift them into the dish. Sprinkle the flour over the juices left in the pan and cook for a minute, blend in the tomatoes, stock, rosemary and seasoning. Bring to the boil, stirring continuously. Stir in beans, taste and check seasoning then pour over chops. Cover with a lid and cook in the oven for about 1½ hours until the meat is tender.

to freeze

Cool, then pack in a rigid container, seal, label and freeze.

to thaw

Thaw at room temperature for about 8 hours, then reheat in the oven at 350°F/180°C/Gas 4 for about 40 minutes until piping hot.

RIGHT: *Lamb Kebabs (page 98)*

Moussaka

It is essential to drain off all surplus fat after frying the lamb.

serves 6

1 lb (450g) uncooked minced shoulder of lamb
8 oz (225g) onions, sliced
2 fat cloves garlic, crushed
1 oz (25g) flour
salt and freshly ground black pepper
14 oz (397g) can tomatoes
2 aubergines

sauce
1 oz (25g) butter
1 oz (25g) flour
½ pint (300ml) milk
1 teaspoon Dijon mustard
a little grated nutmeg
salt and freshly ground black pepper
3 oz (75g) well flavoured Cheddar cheese, grated
1 egg, beaten

Cook lamb in a non-stick pan over a low heat to let the fat run out, drain, and then add onions and garlic. Increase heat and fry quickly until meat is browned. Stir in flour, seasoning and tomatoes, bring to the boil and simmer for about 5 minutes. Slice aubergines and blanch in boiling salted water for about 1 minute to soften the skins and stop discoloration. Drain dry on kitchen paper.

To make the sauce, melt butter in a pan then stir in flour and cook for about 1 minute then gradually blend in milk and bring to the boil, stirring well. Add mustard, nutmeg, seasoning and cheese. Remove from heat then stir in egg when cooled slightly. Mix well.

To assemble, spread half the meat mixture over bottom of a large, greased ovenproof dish, cover with half the aubergines, season and repeat with remaining meat and aubergines. Pour over the cheese sauce.

to serve now
Heat oven to 350°F/180°C/Gas 4. Cook moussaka uncovered for 45 minutes to an hour until golden brown.

to freeze
Freeze uncooked, the dish over-wrapped in foil, sealed and labelled.

to thaw
Uncover, thaw at room temperature for about 6 hours then cook as above.

LEFT: *Moussaka (above)*

Lamb Kebabs

Fillet of lamb is inexpensive—from the scrag and middle end of neck of lamb—and is beautifully lean and tender. You could also use fillet of pork or breast of chicken. The marinade tenderises the meat as well as adding flavour, and it goes on doing so in the freezer.

serves 4 | *¾ lb (350g) lamb fillet*

marinade
4 tablespoons olive oil
2 fat cloves garlic, crushed
1 tablespoon white wine vinegar
1 small onion, chopped

for serving only
2 medium sized onions, cut into 8 pieces
4 oz (100g) button mushrooms
1 red pepper, cored, seeded and cut into 1 inch (2.5cm) pieces

Cut lamb into neat bite-sized chunks. Put lamb in a bowl with marinade ingredients. Cover with cling film and leave in the refrigerator overnight if cooking straight away.

to serve now
Lift lamb out of marinade and arrange on 4 flat skewers with the onion, mushrooms and pepper. Heat grill, brush kebabs with marinade and grill on a wire rack in the grill pan for about 15 minutes until the lamb is cooked. Keep turning the kebabs and brushing them with marinade during cooking. Serve with a green salad and perhaps saffron rice.

to freeze
Freeze lamb in marinade in a polythene container.

to thaw
Thaw overnight in the refrigerator, then assemble kebabs and cook as above.

Lamb and Celery Casserole

Serve this tasty casserole with lots of mashed potato to mop up the gravy.

serves 3-4
2 tablespoons sunflower oil
1 lb (450g) lamb neck fillet, sliced
1 oz (25g) flour
1 pint (600ml) good stock
2 onions, chopped
2 carrots, chopped
4 sticks celery, chopped
salt
freshly ground black pepper
1 bayleaf
a little gravy browning

Heat the oven to 325°F/160°C/Gas 3.

Heat the oil in a large casserole dish and fry the meat quickly to brown, then remove from the dish. Stir the flour into the fat remaining in the dish, cook for 1 minute, then stir in the stock. Return meat to the dish with the vegetables, seasoning, bayleaf and gravy browning. Cover and cook in the oven until tender (about 2 hours). Taste and adjust the seasoning and remove the bayleaf.

to freeze
Turn into a rigid container, cool, cover, label and freeze.

to thaw
Thaw overnight in the refrigerator. Reheat in a pan for about 10 minutes until piping hot.

Special Roast Chicken

Freeze a *fresh* chicken for up to a month. When thawed, stuff the breast end with this stuffing (which can also be stored in the freezer). Serve with a good gravy made with the juices from the roasting tin plus a little orange juice and stock. The stuffing is deliciously orangey.

serves 6

4 lb (1.7kg) fresh chicken
1 chicken stock cube
6 fl. oz (175ml) orange juice
2 oz (50g) easy-cook, long-grain rice
3oz (25g) butter
1 small onion, finely chopped
2 sticks celery, finely chopped
1 oz (25g) blanched almonds, chopped
2 oz (50g) dried apricots, soaked overnight and chopped
2 tablespoons freshly chopped parsley
salt and freshly ground black pepper

for serving only
1 oz (25g) butter

To prepare the stuffing, crumble the stock cube into orange juice and bring to the boil in a pan. Stir in rice, cover with a lid and simmer for about 20 minutes. Draw aside and leave to stand for about 5 minutes for the rice to absorb the remaining liquid.

Heat 1 oz (25g) of the butter in a pan and quickly sauté the onion and celery for about 5 minutes until tender. Remove from the heat and stir in almonds, apricots, parsley, seasoning and rice.

to serve now

Remove giblets from the bird and use for stock for gravy (or freeze). Stuff the breast end of the bird with rice stuffing and secure skin firmly over the stuffing with small skewers. Heat the oven to 375°F/190°C/Gas 5. Spread chicken with remaining butter, season, and roast in the oven for about 1½ hours until the chicken is cooked, basting occasionally.

to freeze

Freeze chicken and stuffing separately before roasting; the chicken wrapped in cling film, the stuffing in a small container. Seal and label.

to thaw

Thaw at a cool room temperature overnight, or in the refrigerator for 24 hours, then stuff and roast as suggested above.

Chicken en Surprise

This casseroled chicken in a mild curried parsnip sauce is interesting, and well worth trying.

serves 6

1 oz (25g) butter
1 tablespoon sunflower oil
6 chicken portions, skin removed
4 oz (100g) onion, chopped
1 large parsnip, cubed
1 fat clove garlic, crushed
1 oz (25g) flour
1 rounded teaspoon curry powder
1 pint (600ml) good chicken stock
salt and freshly ground black pepper

for serving only
¼ pint (150ml) single cream
snipped chives

Heat the oven to 325°F/160°C/Gas 3.

Melt butter and oil in a large pan, add chicken joints and fry for about 10 minutes until browned all over. Lift out with a slotted spoon and arrange in a 3 pint (1.7 litre) casserole dish. Leave on one side.

Add onion, parsnip and garlic to the fat left in the bottom of the pan and fry gently for about 10 minutes until beginning to soften. Stir in the flour and curry powder and cook for a minute, then add the stock and the seasoning and bring to the boil, stirring all the time. Once thickened, cover pan with a lid and simmer gently for about 20 minutes until the parsnip is tender. Purée this sauce in a processor or blender until smooth then pour over the chicken joints. Cover casserole with a lid and cook in the oven for about 1 hour until the chicken is cooked.

to serve now

Check seasoning then stir in cream and sprinkle with chives.

to freeze

Freeze cooled chicken in a rigid container without cream. Seal and label.

to thaw

Thaw at room temperature for about 8 hours then reheat, uncovered, in the oven at 350°F/180°C/Gas 4 for about 30 minutes until heated right through. Add the cream and chives as above.

Chicken and Celery à la Crème

A light supper dish, which is delicious served with fresh green broccoli.

serves 6

2 oz (50g) butter
6 chicken joints, skinned
6 sticks celery, sliced
8 oz (225g) carrots, peeled and sliced
1½ oz (40g) flour
1 pint (600ml) milk
1 chicken stock cube
salt
freshly ground black pepper

Melt butter in a large pan and fry chicken joints for about 10 minutes until lightly browned. Turn once during cooking. Lift out on to a plate with a slotted spoon.

Add the vegetables to the fat left in the pan and fry until golden brown. Stir in the flour and cook for 2 minutes, then gradually add the milk, stirring all the time until thickened. Crumble in the stock cube and add seasoning. Lift the chicken joints back into the pan, cover with a lid and simmer for about 45 minutes until the chicken is tender.

to freeze

Allow to cool, turn into a rigid container, seal, label and freeze.

to thaw

Thaw at room temperature for about 5 hours then reheat thoroughly in a large pan. Serve with a little chopped parsley sprinkled on top.

Chicken Tagliatelle Casserole

For 6 people you can get away with using a smaller chicken or add the last cuts of a large roast chicken instead.

serves 6-8
3½ lb (1.5kg) chicken
4 oz (100g) onion, chopped
1 bayleaf
salt and freshly ground black pepper
4 oz (100g) green pepper, chopped
4 oz (100g) mushrooms, sliced
10 oz (295g) can condensed cream of mushroom soup
1 tablespoon freshly chopped parsley
12 oz (350g) ribbon noodles
6 oz (175g) Cheddar cheese, grated

Put chicken in a pan just big enough to hold it with 1 pint (600ml) water, a little of the chopped onion, the bayleaf, and seasoning. Bring to boil, cover and simmer for about an hour until tender. Remove chicken, strain off liquid, discarding onion and bayleaf, and allow to cool. Skim and save fat off liquid.

Put some chicken fat in a pan and sauté remaining onion until tender then add pepper and mushrooms. Cook for about 5 minutes until beginning to soften. Cut chicken into bite-sized pieces, discarding skin and bones, and add to vegetable mixture. Stir in can of soup plus a canful of the chicken stock, plus the chopped parsley, and simmer gently for 5 minutes. While this is cooking put noodles on to boil in salted water, cook until just tender, then drain.

Put ⅓ of the sauce mixture in the bottom of a 3 pint (1.7 litre) shallow casserole dish. Top with half the noodles, then half remaining sauce, then noodles, and lastly the sauce. Top with grated cheese.

to serve now
Cook in the oven at 425°F/220°C/Gas 7 for about 15 minutes until bubbling, or brown under a hot grill.

to freeze
Freeze without cooking in oven. Wrap casserole dish in foil, seal well and label.

to thaw
Thaw at room temperature for about 8 hours then bake at 325°F/160°C/Gas 3 for about 1 hour.

Chicken Pilaff

A pilaff freezes well but is best used within a month. It is improved after reheating by forking in a little butter.

serves 6-8
2 large onions, chopped
1 fat clove garlic, crushed
1 large red pepper, seeded and sliced
2oz (50g) butter
12 oz (350g) long-grain rice
1¾ pints (1 litre) chicken stock
1 teaspoon curry powder
1 tablespoon freshly chopped herbs
4 oz (100g) mushrooms, sliced
12 oz (350g) cooked chicken, diced
4 oz (100g) frozen peas
7oz (175g) can sweetcorn, drained
salt
freshly ground black pepper

Fry the onion, garlic and red pepper in 1½ oz (40g) butter for about 5 minutes or until soft. Add the rice and fry for 2 minutes, stirring. Stir in the stock, curry powder and herbs. Bring to the boil, cover and simmer for about 25 minutes until the rice is tender and all the liquid has been absorbed.

Fry the mushrooms in the remaining butter until just tender. Stir the mushrooms, chicken pieces, peas and corn into the rice mixture and season to taste.

to freeze Turn into lidded foil containers, cool, cover, seal, label and freeze.

to thaw Thaw at room temperature for about 7 hours. Remove the lids, cover lightly with foil and reheat in the oven at 325°F/160°C/Gas 3 for about 45 minutes, stirring occasionally with a fork.

Mediterranean Chicken

If liked, the skin on the chicken can be removed before frying. The last little bone of the wing and leg can be cut off to make a neater joint, this being done after they are cooked.

serves 4

1 oz (25g) butter
1 tablespoon sunflower oil
4 chicken joints
4 oz (100g) onion, chopped
1 green pepper, seeded and sliced
14 oz (397g) can tomatoes
4 oz (100g) mushrooms, quartered
¼ pint (150ml) chicken stock
salt
freshly ground black pepper
a little sugar

for serving only
2 tablespoons freshly chopped parsley.

Heat the butter and oil in a large frying pan. Add chicken joints and onion and fry for about 5 minutes, turning the joints until they are a pale golden brown on all sides.

Drain off any excess fat and then add all remaining ingredients to the pan. Bring to the boil, cover with a lid or piece of foil and simmer gently for about 30 minutes until the chicken is tender. Taste and adjust seasoning.

to freeze

Turn into a rigid container, cover, seal, label and freeze.

to thaw

Thaw overnight in the refrigerator. Heat oven to 400°F/200°C/Gas 6. Turn chicken into an ovenproof dish and cook in the oven for about 40 minutes until piping hot. Before serving skim off any fat which may have formed on surface and sprinkle with parsley.

Sweet and Sour Chicken Thighs

Chicken thighs are meaty even though they are small. I always consider them a better buy than drumsticks.

serves 4

1 oz (25g) butter
1 tablespoon sunflower oil
6 chicken thighs
8 oz (225g) can pineapple pieces, drained and juice reserved
1 medium onion, sliced
1 level tablespoon cornflour
3 teaspoons light muscovado sugar
1 tablespoon soy sauce
2 tablespoons tomato ketchup
2 tablespoons white wine vinegar
¼ pint (150ml) good stock
salt
freshly ground black pepper

Measure the butter and oil into a large non-stick frying pan, and fry thighs quickly until evenly browned (about 5 minutes). With a slotted spoon, lift chicken into a 2 pint (1.2 litre) shallow casserole dish. Add pineapple pieces to the dish.

Fry onion in fat left in pan until golden brown. Meanwhile mix cornflour, sugar, soy sauce, ketchup and vinegar in a bowl, and stir in pineapple juice, stock and cooked onion. Season well then pour over the chicken and pineapple pieces.

to serve now

Heat the oven to 350°F/180°C/Gas 4. Cover casserole dish with a lid, and cook in the oven for about an hour until the chicken is tender.

to freeze

Freeze without cooking in the oven, the dish wrapped well with cling film, sealed and labelled.

to thaw

Thaw overnight in the refrigerator then cook as above.

Family Chicken Pie

A good way of using up either cooked chicken or turkey. You could also freeze the pie complete, before baking.

serves 4

2oz (50g) butter
8 oz (225g) carrots, diced
6 sticks celery, chopped
1 oz (25g) flour
½ pint (300ml) milk
salt
freshly ground black pepper
juice of ½ lemon
8 oz (225g) cooked chicken, cut into small pieces
4 oz (100g) cooked ham or bacon, cut into small pieces

for serving only
8 oz (227g) packet frozen puff pastry thawed

Melt the butter in a pan and gently fry carrots and celery for about 10 minutes until just beginning to soften, then stir in the flour. Cook for 1 minute, then gradually add the milk. Bring to the boil, stirring, and simmer for about 3 minutes then add the remaining ingredients and mix well.

to serve now
Turn into a 1 pint (600ml) pie dish. Roll out the pastry and cover the pie. Use the trimmings to decorate the top. Brush with milk and bake at 425°F/220°C/Gas 7 for about 15 minutes, then reduce the oven temperature to 350°F/180°C/Gas 4 for a further 15 minutes.

to freeze
Freeze filling on its own in a rigid container, covered, sealed and labelled.

to thaw
Leave filling to thaw at room temperature for about 4 hours, assemble and cook pie as above.

Turkey in Cider Sauce

An excellent way of using up the last cuts of left-over turkey with some mushrooms.

serves 4

1 lb (450g) left-over turkey
2 oz (50g) butter
2 onions, chopped
1½ oz (40g) flour
½ pint (300ml) dry cider
½ pint (300ml) milk
6 oz (175g) mushrooms, quartered
salt
freshly ground black pepper

Cut the turkey into bite-sized pieces.

Melt the butter in a pan, add the onions, and fry for about 5 minutes until tender. Stir in the flour and cook for a further minute before stirring in the cider and milk. Bring to the boil, stirring, and once thickened, add mushrooms and seasoning as well as the turkey. Cook for about 10 minutes until heated right through.

to freeze

Turn into a rigid container, cool, seal, label and freeze.

to thaw

Thaw overnight in the refrigerator. Turn into a casserole and cook at 350°F/180°C/Gas 4 for about 40 minutes until piping hot. Serve with boiled rice.

Braised Oxtail

This dish takes at least 4 hours to cook as the oxtail is one of the toughest parts of the animal yet one of the most delicious. Very often I double up on this recipe and eat one oxtail now and freeze the other for later. There will be plenty of gravy with this dish, so there may be enough left over to serve as soup.

serves 6

3 lb (1.3kg) oxtail, in pieces
knob of lard or dripping
2 onions, chopped
2 large carrots, chopped
8 sticks celery, chopped
2 rashers streaky bacon, chopped
1 oz (25g) flour
2 bayleaves
3 sprigs parsley
plenty of freshly ground black pepper
salt
2 pints (1.1 litre) good beef stock

Trim off any excess fat from the oxtail joints. Heat the lard or the dripping in a pan, add the oxtail and brown on all sides, then remove from the pan. Add the vegetables and the bacon to the pan, and cook gently for about 5 minutes. Stir in the flour and cook for a minute, then blend in the remaining ingredients and bring to the boil, stirring until thickened slightly.

Return the oxtail to the pan, cover and simmer for about 4 hours or until the meat can be easily removed from the bone. Take care to skim off every scrap of fat once the oxtail is cooked (best done when the dish has cooled and the fat has set on the top).

to freeze   Cool then pack in a rigid container, seal, label and freeze.

to thaw   Thaw at room temperature for about 8 hours then reheat gently in a pan until piping hot.

Countryman's Rabbit

Rabbit is one of the less expensive meats and when cooked in this way is rather good. The pork streaky slices enrich the dish, but you could use 4 oz (100g) bacon pieces instead (often available on the delicatessen counter).

serves 4-6
4 pork streaky slices
1 rabbit, jointed
1 onion, chopped
4 sticks celery, sliced
10½ oz (300g) can condensed celery soup
¼ pint (150ml) cider
1 tablespoon freshly chopped parsley
salt
freshly ground black pepper

Heat oven to 350°F/180°C/Gas 4.

Put pork in a non-stick pan and heat gently until fat begins to run, then increase heat and fry until browned all over. Lift out of pan into a 3 pint (1.7 litre) casserole. Add rabbit to pan and fry until browned all over, lift into casserole with a slotted spoon.

Fry onion in fat remaining in pan for about 5 minutes until soft, then stir in remaining ingredients and pour over the rabbit. Cover casserole with a lid and cook in the oven for about 1½ hours until the meat is tender.

to freeze   Turn into a rigid container, cool, cover, seal, label and freeze.

to thaw   Thaw overnight in the refrigerator then reheat in the oven in a covered casserole at 350°F/180°C/Gas 4 for about 30 minutes.

Jugged Hare

Hare is still inexpensive to buy, and it's a delicious dish to have in the freezer.

serves 6

8 oz (225g) *prunes*
1 *good sized hare, jointed*
2 oz (50g) *seasoned flour*
2 oz (50g) *dripping*
8 oz (225g) *onion, chopped*
1 *pint (600ml) good stock*
¼ *pint (150ml) port*
2 *good tablespoons redcurrant jelly*
salt
freshly ground black pepper

Soak prunes in water overnight, then cut in half and remove and discard stones. Heat oven to 325°F/160°C/Gas 3.

Toss the hare joints in seasoned flour until well coated. Heat dripping in a large lidded heatproof and ovenproof pan and fry the joints until browned all over. Lift joints on to a plate with a slotted spoon and leave on one side. Fry onion in fat left in the pan until browned then add any remaining flour from coating the joints. Cook for a minute then gradually blend in the stock, port, jelly, seasoning and prunes. Bring to the boil, stirring all the time, then lift joints back into the pan. Bring sauce back to boiling point, then remove to the oven. Cook for about 3 hours until the meat is tender.

to freeze   Allow to cool then turn into a rigid container, seal, label and freeze.

to thaw   Thaw at room temperature for about 8 hours then heat in a pan for about 20 minutes until heated right through.

Pheasant with Grapes

A very good way of serving older pheasants. Pigeons or other game birds would be good served similarly.

serves 6-8
brace of pheasants
1 oz (25g) butter
1 tablespoon sunflower oil
1 large onion, chopped
1 oz (25g) flour
¾ pint (450ml) white wine
1 chicken stock cube
1 tablespoon redcurrant jelly
1 Bramley apple, chopped
salt and freshly ground black pepper

for serving only
8 oz (225g) green grapes, halved and seeded

Heat the oven to 325°F/160°C/Gas 3.

Fry pheasants in butter and oil in a large pan until browned all over, then lift out into a 3 pint (1.7 litre) casserole dish. Fry onion in fat left in the pan until golden brown, then stir in flour and cook for 1 minute. Gradually blend in wine, stirring until thickened, then add stock cube, jelly, apple and seasoning. Pour sauce over pheasants and cook in oven for 1-3 hours (depending on age) until tender.

to serve now
Lift out birds and when cool enough to handle, joint them and arrange on a warmed serving dish. Pour over the sauce and serve garnished with grapes. Skim any fat from the top of sauce before serving or freezing.

to freeze
Freeze jointed, with sauce, in a sealed, and carefully labelled container, without grapes.

to thaw
Thaw at room temperature for about 10 hours then reheat in the oven at 350°F/180°C/Gas 4 for about 40 minutes until piping hot. Garnish as above.

Highland Venison

If you're lucky enough to find some venison, this is a deliciously tender dish.

serves 6   *1½ lb (675g) stewing venison*

marinade
½ pint (300ml) red wine
2 bayleaves
8 peppercorns
2 cloves garlic, split in 4
4 tablespoons sunflower oil
1 onion, sliced

sauce
4 oz (100g) fatty bacon, cubed
3 oz (75g) German smoked sausage, skinned and sliced
1 large onion, chopped
generous 1 oz (25g) flour
about ½ pint (300ml) good stock
bouquet garni
1 tablespoon bramble jelly
salt
freshly ground black pepper
dash gravy browning

Cut venison into cubes about ¾ inch (2cm) square. Leave in marinade for 24 hours in the refrigerator. Lift meat out of marinade, remove and discard peppercorns, bayleaf, onion and garlic, strain wine and reserve.

For the sauce, put the bacon into a non-stick frying pan, and cook slowly to draw out the fat. Add the sliced sausage and onion, and cook for about 10 minutes until the bacon is crispy. Add flour and blend well. Make reserved marinade up to 1 pint (600ml) with stock, stir into the pan and bring to the boil, stirring. Add the venison, bouquet garni and bramble jelly. Season well, add gravy browning, cover and simmer very gently for about 2½ hours until tender.

to freeze   Cool then turn into a rigid container, cover, seal, label and freeze.

to thaw   Thaw at room temperature for about 8 hours then turn into a pan and reheat gently until piping hot.

Pizza

makes 3 large pizzas	A brown-bread based pizza is extra delicious and it gives a rather nutty flavour. Make brown bread mix up as directed on a 1 lb 14 oz (850g) packet then divide into 3 equal portions and roll out each piece on a large baking sheet to a 10 inch (25cm) round. Brush with a little oil, choose a topping from the three below, then leave the 'filled' pizzas to prove in a warm place for about 30 minutes.

Classic pizza

2 tablespoons sunflower oil
1 large onion, chopped
14 oz (397g) can tomatoes, drained and roughly chopped
¼ teaspoon dried mixed herbs
salt and freshly ground black pepper
3 oz (75g) Emmenthal cheese
anchovy fillets

Heat oil and quickly fry onion for about 5 minutes until beginning to soften then stir in the tomatoes, herbs and seasoning. Cook gently until the mixture has reduced to a thick pulp. Spread over the dough base, and arrange slices of cheese and a lattice of anchovy fillets on top.

Bacon and mushroom pizza

1 oz (25g) butter
8 rashers streaky bacon, chopped
4 oz (100g) button mushrooms, sliced
4 oz (100g) Cheddar cheese, grated

Melt butter, add the bacon and mushrooms, and cook for about 5 minutes. Drain and arrange on the dough, cover with grated cheese.

Tuna pizza

8 tablespoons tomato chutney
6oz (175g) tuna fish, drained and flaked
¼ teaspoon dried mixed herbs
2 large tomatoes, sliced

Mix chutney, fish and herbs well. Spread over dough base, and arrange tomato slices on top.

to freeze Open freeze until firm then lift off baking sheets and wrap in a double thickness of foil. Label and return to the freezer.

to thaw Unwrap, place on a lightly oiled baking tray and bake in the oven at 425°F/220°C/Gas 7 for about 30 minutes.

Lasagne

An Italian classic and a marvellous dish for the freezer.

serves 8

6 oz (175g) lasagne (the kind that requires no pre cooking)
2 oz (50g) each of Cheddar cheese and Gruyère cheese, grated
1 oz (25g) Parmesan cheese, grated

spaghetti sauce
2 oz (50g) bacon pieces, chopped
2 lb (900g) lean raw minced beef
1½oz (40g) flour
6 sticks celery chopped
12 oz (350g) onion, chopped
½ pint (300 ml) stock
2 fat cloves garlic, crushed
14 oz (397g) can tomatoes and 4 good tablespoons tomato purée
1 teaspoon sugar
1 teaspoon fresh thyme, chopped
salt and freshly ground black pepper

white sauce
2oz (50g) butter
1½oz (40g) flour
1 pint (600 ml) milk
1 teaspoon Dijon mustard and a little ground nutmeg
salt and freshly ground black pepper

First prepare the spaghetti sauce. Put the bacon in a non-stick pan and fry gently until fat begins to run, then add mince. Increase heat and fry quickly until browned, then add flour and blend well. Stir in all the remaining ingredients, bring to the boil and cover with a lid. Simmer for about an hour until meat is tender. Meanwhile make white sauce in usual way with butter, flour and milk. When thickened, remove from heat and stir in mustard, nutmeg and seasoning.

In a 9 x 12 inch (23 x 30 cm) shallow ovenproof dish put layers of spaghetti sauce, lasagne, white sauce then cheese. Repeat this, finishing with cheese sprinkled on top. Do not overlap the lasagne—if necessary break the pieces to fit into the dish.

to freeze

Leave until cold, cover, label and freeze.

to thaw

Thaw at room temperature for about 12 hours. Cook uncovered at 375°F/190°C/Gas 5 for about 45-60 minutes until heated through.

Swedish Pancakes

It seemed sensible to make this recipe into two meals for four as there are two sauces *as well as* pancakes!

**makes
2 meals
for 4**

8 oz (225g) plain flour
2 eggs
2 tablespoons sunflower oil
1 pint (600ml) milk

cheese sauce
2 oz (50g) butter
2 oz (50g) flour
1 pint (600ml) milk
6 oz (175g) well flavoured Cheddar cheese
1 teaspoon Dijon mustard
salt
freshly ground black pepper

spaghetti sauce *(see previous recipe)*

First prepare the pancakes. Put flour in a bowl, blend in the eggs with oil and milk. Heat very little oil in an 8 inch (20cm) pan. Pour 2 tablespoons of the mixture into the pan and tilt and rotate to spread out the batter. Cook for about a minute then turn over and cook the other side for a minute. Turn out and make 15 more pancakes. Stack them interleaved with greaseproof paper until required.

To make the cheese sauce, melt the butter in a pan and stir in the flour. Cook for about a minute then blend in the milk and bring to the boil. Stir until thickened then remove from the heat, and stir in 4 oz (100g) of the cheese, the mustard and seasoning.

Divide the spaghetti sauce between the pancakes and roll up, place in a single layer in two large shallow ovenproof dishes. Pour the cheese sauce over the pancakes and sprinkle with remaining cheese.

to freeze Allow to cool then cover, label and freeze.

to thaw Thaw at room temperature for about 10 hours then bake uncovered in the oven at 400°F/200°C/Gas 6 for about 30 minutes until golden brown.

Mature Cheddar Cheese Croquettes

Good to have ready in the freezer for a quick meal—cook straight from the freezer, no need to thaw.

makes 14

2 oz (50g) block margarine
1 small onion, finely chopped
2 oz (50g) flour
½ pint (300ml) milk
12 oz (350g) mature Cheddar cheese, grated
2 eggs, separated
2 teaspoons Dijon mustard
salt
freshly ground black pepper
little grated nutmeg
2 oz (50g) raspings or brown crumbs

Heat margarine in a pan and fry onion for about 5 minutes until tender. Stir in flour and cook 2 minutes, then gradually blend in milk. Bring to boil, stirring continuously. When thickened, remove from heat, stir in cheese, egg yolks, mustard, seasoning and nutmeg. Chill overnight in the refrigerator then shape into 14 cakes with lightly floured hands.

Lightly beat egg whites and dip cakes firstly into egg white then roll in raspings until coated.

to freeze Open freeze then pack in a rigid container interleaved with greaseproof paper, cover, label and return to freezer.

to thaw Cook straight from frozen. Fry gently in oil for about 10 minutes until sauce is just beginning to melt in centre. Turn once during cooking.

Mushroom Puff Pies

Make straight from the freezer for a quick supper when the family have had a good lunch.

makes 8

12 oz (350g) button mushrooms, sliced
juice of ½ lemon
salt
freshly ground black pepper
1½ oz (40g) butter
1½ oz (40g) flour
½ pint (300ml) milk
a little ground nutmeg
14 oz (397g) packet bought puff pastry
a little beaten egg

Place the mushrooms and lemon juice in a saucepan and simmer gently for about 5 minutes until the mushrooms are cooked. Season well. Melt the butter in a separate pan, stir in the flour, and cook for 2 minutes. Blend in the milk and bring to the boil. Remove this white sauce from the heat, add the mushroom mixture, and season with nutmeg, salt and pepper.

Roll the pastry out on a floured surface to a 16 x 16 inch (40 x 40cm) square. Divide the pastry into 16 squares. Lift 8 of the squares on to a baking sheet and divide the sauce between them, spooning it into the centre. Brush the edges with beaten egg then lift the other squares on top. Seal the edges well.

to freeze

Open freeze on the baking sheet then lift into a container, label, and return to the freezer.

to thaw

Lift straight from the freezer on to a greased baking sheet, glaze, and bake in a preheated oven (400°F/200°C/Gas 6) for about 20 minutes until golden brown.

Pissaladière

I usually make two of these, one for today and one to freeze raw.

serves 4-6

6 oz (175g) plain flour
1½oz (40g) lard
1½oz (40g) margarine
about 2 tablespoons water

filling
2 tablespoons sunflower oil
2 medium sized onions, sliced
14 oz (397g) can tomatoes
1 clove garlic, crushed
1 good tablespoon tomato purée
1 teaspoon granulated sugar
1 tablespoon freshly chopped mixed herbs
salt and freshly ground black pepper
3 oz (75g) Mozzarella cheese, sliced ⎱ or 4 oz (100g) well
1 oz (25g) grated Parmesan cheese ⎰ flavoured Cheddar, sliced
1¾ oz (45g) can anchovy fillets
a few black olives

Heat the oven to 425°F/220°C/Gas 7. Put the flour in a bowl and rub in the lard and margarine until it resembles fine breadcrumbs. Bind dough with the water, roll out on a lightly floured surface and use to line an 8 inch (20cm) flan tin. Chill for about 20 minutes then bake blind by adding a round of greaseproof paper filled with baking beans, or a piece of foil, for 15-20 minutes. Remove the paper and beans for the last 10 minutes to dry out the flan.

Meanwhile prepare the filling. Heat the oil in a pan, add the onions and fry gently until golden brown, then add the tomatoes, garlic, purée, sugar, herbs, salt and pepper and simmer for about 15 minutes until thick. Arrange the Mozzarella cheese on bottom of flan, sprinkle with Parmesan, and pour the tomato mixture on top. Lay the anchovy fillets in a lattice pattern over the flan and place an olive in each space.

to freeze

Open freeze the flan without further cooking, wrap in a double thickness of foil, seal, label and return to the freezer.

to thaw

Unwrap and thaw at room temperature for about 5 hours. Heat the oven to 375°F/190°C/Gas 5 and bake on a baking sheet for about 30 minutes until the filling is hot and bubbling. Serve with salad.

Cheese and Spinach Quiche

Serve hot with French bread and a crisp salad. To get a brown base to the quiche bake on a thick metal baking sheet that has been preheated in the oven.

serves 4

6oz (175g) plain flour
3 oz (75g) margarine
1½ oz (40g) Parmesan cheese, grated
1 egg yolk
about 1½ tablespoons water

filling
8 oz (225g) packet frozen leaf spinach, thawed and drained
5 oz (150g) carton natural yoghurt
5 oz (150g) carton crème fraîche
1 teaspoon salt
freshly ground black pepper
2 eggs
2 oz (50g) Cheddar cheese, grated

Heat the oven to 422°F/220°C/Gas 7. Heat a baking sheet in the oven.

Put the flour in a bowl and rub in the margarine until like breadcrumbs. Stir in the Parmesan cheese. Mix egg yolk with water and stir into flour to give a firm dough. Roll out on a lightly floured surface and use to line a 9 inch (22.5cm) loose-bottomed flan tin. Chill for 20 minutes. Bake flan case blind using a round piece of greaseproof paper and baking beans or a piece of foil. Stand flan on baking sheet and bake for 20 minutes, removing the paper and beans or foil for the last 10 minutes.

Spread the spinach over the base of the flan. In a bowl mix together the yoghurt, crème fraîche, salt, pepper and eggs, then pour over the spinach and sprinkle with Cheddar cheese. Bake in the oven at 350°F/180°C/Gas 4 for about 20 minutes until the filling is set and a pale golden brown.

to freeze

Open freeze the quiche, then wrap in a double layer of foil, seal, label and return to the freezer.

to thaw

Unwrap and thaw at room temperature for about 4 hours, then reheat in a preheated oven at 350°F/180°C/Gas 4 for 20 minutes.

Swiss Quiche

If no chives are available you could use a couple of spring onions finely sliced.

serves 4

6 oz (175g) plain flour
1½oz (40g) margarine
1½oz (40g) lard
about 2 tablespoons cold water

filling
4 oz (100g) Gruyère cheese, sliced
4 rashers streaky bacon
¼ pint (150ml) single cream
2 large eggs
1 teaspoon freshly chopped parsley
1 teaspoon freshly chopped chives
salt
freshly ground black pepper

Heat the oven to 425°F/220°C/Gas 7 and place a baking sheet in it.

Put the flour in a bowl and rub in the fats until the mixture resembles fine breadcrumbs. Add sufficient cold water to form a firm dough. Roll out the pastry fairly thinly and use to line a 9 inch (22.5cm) loose-bottomed flan tin. Chill in the refrigerator for about 15 minutes.

Line the flan with a piece of greaseproof paper and weigh down with baking beans and bake blind for about 10 minutes. Remove the paper and baking beans, and return to the oven for a further 5 minutes to dry out.

Arrange the slices of cheese in the bottom of the flan. Remove the rind from the bacon and fry gently for about 2 minutes then cut each rasher in half and arrange spoke fashion on top of the cheese. Mix together the cream, eggs and herbs with plenty of seasoning. Pour into the flan case and return to the oven. Reduce the heat to 350°F/180°C/Gas 4 and bake for about 25 minutes or until the filling is set.

to freeze

Open freeze then wrap in foil, seal, label and return to the freezer.

to thaw

Unwrap and thaw at room temperature for about 6 hours. Reheat in the oven at 350°F/180°C/Gas 4 for about 20 minutes.

Ratatouille

A blend of Mediterranean vegetables that may be served hot or cold. Traditionally the vegetables are fried in considerably more oil but I prefer a less oily result.

serves 6

2 small aubergines, sliced
2 courgettes, sliced
salt
4 tablespoons sunflower oil
2 medium sized onions, finely sliced
1 small green pepper, seeded and sliced
1 small red pepper, seeded and sliced
1 clove garlic, crushed
8 oz (225g) tomatoes, peeled and quartered
freshly ground black pepper

for serving only
1 tablespoon chopped parsley

Sprinkle the aubergines and courgettes with 2 tablespoons salt and leave to drain off bitter juices in a colander for 30 minutes. Thereafter rinse in cold water and dry on kitchen paper.

Heat the oil in a large pan, add the onions and cook gently until they are soft (about 10 minutes). Add dried aubergines and courgettes, with the red and green peppers and garlic. Cover with a lid and simmer for 30 minutes, stirring occasionally. Add the tomatoes to the pan with plenty of seasoning and cook for a further 10 minutes or until all the vegetables are cooked.

to freeze   Turn into a rigid container, cool, cover, label and freeze.

to thaw   Thaw at room temperature for about 8 hours and serve either hot as a vegetable—in a warm serving dish, sprinkled with parsley—or cold as an hors d'oeuvre.

COLD PUDDINGS
AND ICES

It is very important to pack these well. Icecreams are best
turned into shallow square or oblong containers filled to about
¾ inch (1.75cm) from the brim, then covered with a well
fitting lid. If they are only half full the top layer of the
icecream deteriorates quickly.

If you want to freeze mousses and cheesecakes and individual
puddings, choose toughened glass or ceramic dishes with
straight or convex sides: this means that as they freeze and they
expand, the dish won't break.

It is difficult to give exact thawing time for cold dishes, as it
depends, of course, on how dense the pudding is: a 6 inch (15
cm) deep 2 pint (litre) mousse will take twice as long to thaw
as a very shallow dish of the same capacity.

Lemon Icecream

A lovely rich yellow colour and has a good lemon flavour too.

serves 8

4 eggs, separated
½ pint (300ml) double cream, whipped
8 fl. oz (225ml) lemon curd, preferably home-made
2oz (50g) icing sugar, sieved

Whisk the egg yolks until blended then stir in the cream and lemon curd.

In a separate, larger bowl, whisk the egg whites until stiff, then whisk in the sugar a teaspoonful at a time, beating well after each addition.

Fold the lemon mixture into the egg whites until well mixed then turn into a 2½ pint (1.4 litre) container.

to freeze Cover firmly, label and freeze until solid.

to thaw Leave to thaw at room temperature for about 10 minutes before serving.

Very Special Ginger Icecream

Stem ginger is often sitting on the larder shelf in the jar from one Christmas to the next. This is the perfect way of serving it with brandy snaps. I cheat and buy these at Marks and Spencer's!

serves 8
4 eggs, separated
1 level teaspoon ground ginger
4 oz (100g) stem ginger, chopped
4oz (100g) caster sugar
½ pint (300ml) whipping cream

Whisk yolks and both gingers in a small bowl until blended. In a larger bowl whisk the egg whites with an electric whisk until stiff, then whisk in the sugar a teaspoonful at a time. The whites will get stiffer and stiffer as the sugar is added. Blend in the yolks and ginger until no streaks of colour remain. Whisk the cream until it forms peaks and fold into the ginger mixture.

to freeze   Turn into a 2½ pint (1.4 litre) container. Cover, label and freeze until solid.

to thaw   Leave to thaw at room temperature for 5 minutes then serve in scoops in small glasses with brandy snaps.

Fresh Grapefruit Sherbet

This has a wonderful taste and texture, and might be even more special served in half grapefruit skins (the flesh served for breakfast) which have been chilled in the freezer as well.

serves 4
finely grated rind and strained juice of 2 grapefruit
¼ pint (150ml) double cream, whipped
2 egg whites
4oz (100g) caster sugar

Mix the rind, juice and cream together in a bowl. Whisk the egg whites with an electric hand held whisk or a rotary whisk until stiff and then whisk in the sugar a teaspoonful at a time. Fold into the cream.

to freeze
Turn into an ice-cube tray and leave in the freezer for 2 hours, then remove and beat well in a bowl with a wooden spoon. Return to the tray and the freezer for a further 4 hours.

to thaw
Take out of freezer 5 minutes before serving in scoops in small ramekin dishes, decorated with fresh mint. Or as suggested above.

Baked Alaska

A great favourite with many children as well as adults, this freezes well for up to 2 weeks. I often make one for a children's birthday party and the moment it comes out of the oven I quickly fix some of those new long very thin candles firmly into the pudding then light them and rush to the table! This I find the children really love, as a traditional birthday cake tends to linger in the tin for a couple of weeks. I make it from bought ingredients, but one could make a more sophisticated one for adults using home-made icecream and sponge base.

serves 6

1 raspberry Swiss roll
2 tablespoons sherry
2 egg whites
4 oz (100g) caster sugar
1 lb (450g) block raspberry ripple icecream

Cut the Swiss roll into 7 slices and arrange them on an 8 inch (20 cm) pie plate so that there is one slice in the centre and the other 6 form a circle around and touching it. Sprinkle with the sherry.

Whisk the egg whites until they are stiff, then add the sugar a teaspoon at a time, whisking well after each addition. Scoop the icecream on to the swiss roll slices, shaping it into a round. Cover quickly with the meringue.

to freeze

Open freeze, then carefully wrap in cling film. Use within 2 weeks.

to thaw

Thaw at room temperature for about 10 minutes while the oven is heating (to 425°F/220°C/Gas 7) then bake the pudding for about 5 minutes until a very pale golden brown. Serve at once.

Lemon Frosties

Serve cut in slices like a cheesecake, with fresh strawberries.

serves 8

3 oz (75g) Frosties, crushed
1½ oz (40g) butter, melted

lemon filling
2 eggs, separated
7 oz (196g) can condensed milk
finely grated rind and juice of 2 lemons

Put the Frosties in a bowl then stir in the melted butter until thoroughly blended. Press half this mixture over the base of a 7 inch (17.5cm) square cake tin.

To make the filling, beat the egg yolks until creamy then blend in the condensed milk, lemon rind and juice, until the mixture thickens. Whisk the egg whites with an electric hand or rotary whisk until stiff and fold into the lemon mixture. Turn into the cake tin and smooth the top. Cover with the remaining Frostie mixture, pressing lightly on top.

to freeze   Wrap tin with cling film, and freeze until firm.

to thaw   Leave to stand at room temperature for about 5 minutes, then turn out of tin and serve.

RIGHT: *Chicken Pilaff (page 104) and Garlic Herb Loaf (page 44)*

Chocolate Bombes

These are chocolate cases filled with cassata icecream. It is essential to use wax- or silicone-treated paper cake cases.

serves 6

8oz (225g) plain chocolate
6 paper cases (see above)

filling
2 eggs
2oz (50g) caster sugar
¼ pint (150ml) double cream
4 oz (100g) glacé fruits, chopped
a little Cointreau to taste

Break the chocolate into pieces into a bowl, stand over a pan of simmering water, and leave until melted. Do not allow the chocolate to get too hot. Coat the insides of 6 strong cases with the chocolate, using the handle of a teaspoon to make a smooth even coating, then allow to set.

Separate the eggs and whisk the yolks until well blended. Whisk the whites until stiff then whisk in the sugar a teaspoonful at a time. Whisk the cream until it holds soft peaks, then fold into the egg whites with the yolks, glacé fruits and Cointreau. Divide the mixture between the moulds and smooth the tops.

to freeze Cover each with a piece of foil, seal, label, and freeze.

to thaw Thaw at room temperature for about 5 minutes, then gently remove paper cases and serve individually.

LEFT: *Devon Apple Pie (page 156)*

Lemon Cream Icebox Pudding

This pudding is very rich, so it is best served in thin wedges.

serves 6-8
4oz (100g) butter
6oz (175g) caster sugar
4 eggs, separated
grated rind and juice of 2 large lemons
2 packets sponge fingers

for serving only
¼ pint (150ml) whipped cream
lemon slices

Line a 6 inch (15 cm) round cake tin with cling film.

Cream butter with sugar until light and creamy, then beat in the egg yolks with lemon rind and juice until well blended. In a separate bowl whisk egg whites with a rotary or electric whisk until stiff then fold into lemon mixture.

Arrange a layer of sponge fingers sugar side down in bottom of tin then a good layer of the lemon filling. Repeat this, finishing with a layer of sponge fingers on top. Chill until set.

to freeze
Freeze when set, and before decorating. Cover well with cling film or foil, seal and label.

to thaw
Thaw overnight in the refrigerator then turn out on to a serving plate and decorate with whipped cream and lemon slices.

Jen's Chocolate Torte

This, too, is very rich. Serve with a little single pouring cream.

serves 6-8
3 oz (75g) butter, softened
3 oz (75g) caster sugar
2 oz (50g) cocoa, sieved
1 egg yolk
2 tablespoons sherry
2 oz (50g) walnuts, chopped
2 packets sponge fingers
¹/₈ pint (75ml) black coffee

for serving only
¼ pint (150ml) whipping cream, whipped
chocolate flake

Line an 8 inch (20cm) deep round cake tin with cling film.

Beat butter and sugar together until light and creamy then stir in the cocoa, egg yolk, sherry and nuts. Mix well together to give a spreading consistency.

Dip the sponge fingers, non sugar side down, quickly in the coffee, arrange a layer in the bottom of the tin, sugar side towards the tin and cover with half the chocolate filling. Arrange another layer of coffee dipped fingers on top and spread with remaining filling, then cover with remaining fingers, sugar side uppermost. Chill until set.

to freeze Cover with foil, seal and label.

to thaw Turn out on to a serving dish and thaw in the refrigerator overnight, then cover the sides with whipped cream and decorate with broken chocolate flake.

Quick Lemon Cheesecake

This cheesecake is quick (made in 10 minutes), delicious, and it freezes well.

serves 6

2 oz (50g) butter
4 oz (100g) digestive biscuits, crushed
1 oz (25g) demerara sugar
8 oz (225g) cream cheese
¼ pint (150ml) double cream
7 oz (196g) can condensed milk
grated rind and juice of 2 lemons

Melt the butter in a pan then stir in the biscuit crumbs and the sugar. Mix well then turn into a deep 7 inch (17.5cm) pie plate and press into shape around the base and sides of the plate with the back of a spoon.

Place the cream cheese in a bowl, cream until soft then beat in the cream and condensed milk. Slowly add the lemon rind and juice. Pour mixture into the flan case.

to freeze   Wrap the cheesecake, including plate, in cling film, label and freeze.

to thaw   Thaw overnight in the refrigerator. Garnish each serving with a twist of lemon.

Rum and Raisin Chocolate Cheesecake

Quite a long and involved recipe, but well worth it for a special occasion. Start the night before by soaking the raisins in the rum.

cuts into 10 wedges

2½ oz (65g) butter
2 oz (50g) demerara sugar
5 oz (150g) digestive biscuits, crushed

cheesecake filling
1 teaspoon instant coffee
2 level tablespoons cocoa
3 tablespoons boiling water
2 eggs, seperated, the whites stiffly beaten
2 oz (50g) caster sugar
½ oz (15g) powdered gelatine dissolved in 3 tablespoons cold water
8 oz (225g) Philadelphia cream cheese
¼ pint (150ml) whipping cream, lightly whipped
2 oz (50g) raisins soaked in 4 tablespoons rum overnight

for serving only
¼ pint (150ml) whipping cream, whipped
chocolate flake or drops

To make the crumb crust, melt butter and stir in sugar and biscuit crumbs until blended. Press into a 9 inch (22.5 cm) flan dish, and put in the refrigerator to harden.

Meanwhile, prepare the filling. In a bowl mix the coffee and cocoa with the boiling water then add the egg yolks and caster sugar. Place the bowl over a pan of hot water and stir until the mixture thickens to coat the back of a spoon (about 10 minutes). Remove from heat. When gelatine and water have formed a sponge, stand the bowl over a pan of simmering water until the gelatine has become quite clear. Remove from the heat and stir into the coffee and cocoa mixture. In a large bowl beat the cream cheese until soft then gradually stir in the cooled cocoa mixture, the whipped cream and the stiffly beaten egg whites. Add the rum and raisins and pour the mixture into the flan case. Refrigerate until set.

to freeze Open freeze in tin, then lift out, wrap in a double thickness of foil, seal, label and return to freezer.

to thaw Thaw at room temperature for about 6 hours after unwrapping. Decorate with whipped cream and chocolate flake or chocolate drops.

Lemon Cream Flan

This is very rich, so serve it cut in small slices.

serves 6

2 oz (50g) butter
10 digestive biscuits, crushed

filling
¼ pint (150ml) lemon cheese
¼ pint (150ml) double cream
7 oz (196g) can condensed milk
juice of 1 large lemon

Melt butter in a pan, remove from heat and stir in biscuit crumbs until well coated. Use to line a 7 inch (17.5cm) loose-bottomed fluted flan tin, pressing firmly over the sides and base.

Beat all the ingredients for the filling together in a bowl until well blended, then pour into the crumb case. (Chill in the refrigerator for about 4 hours if serving, not freezing.)

to freeze Open freeze then remove from the flan tin, wrap in cling film, seal, label and return, carefully, to the freezer.

to thaw Unwrap and allow to defrost in the refrigerator overnight before serving.

Toffee Sponge Flan

Sponge flan cases can be bought quite inexpensively from good supermarkets. I find it useful to have one in the freezer ready to fill or indeed already filled with this toffee mixture.

serves 10

14 oz (397g) can condensed milk
½ pint (300ml) whipping cream
1 rounded teaspoon instant coffee powder
1 oz (25g) caster sugar
1 oz (25g) walnuts, chopped
1 x 12 inch (30cm) sponge flan case

Put the unopened can of condensed milk in a pan and add enough water to cover then simmer gently for about 4 hours. Remember to top up the water occasionally so that it doesn't boil dry. Remove from the heat and allow to cool. Open the can, and the milk will have turned into a toffee-like mixture. Spread this over the base of the flan case.

Whisk together the cream with the coffee and sugar until it stands in soft peaks then spread this over the toffee filling. Decorate with chopped walnuts. Chill well before serving.

to freeze Open freeze quickly then wrap well in cling film, seal, label and return to freezer.

to thaw Remove wrapping and thaw in the refrigerator overnight before serving.

Apple and Almond Tart

Best served cold with lashings of cream.

serves 8

6 oz (175g) plain flour
2 oz (50g) lard
2 oz (50g) margarine
½ oz (15g) caster sugar
2 egg yolks

filling
4oz (100g) marzipan
4 oz (100g) margarine
2 oz (50g) caster sugar
1 lb (450g) cooking apples, peeled and grated
2 egg whites

To make the pastry, put the flour in a bowl, add the fats and rub in until the mixture resembles fine breadcrumbs. Add the sugar and sufficient beaten egg yolk to form a firm dough. Keep the remaining egg yolk for glazing. Roll out the pastry and use to line a 10 inch (25cm) loose-bottomed flan tin. Chill. Keep any pastry trimmings to roll out again and cut into thin strips to use as a lattice. Heat the oven to 425°F/220°C/Gas 7.

Knead the marzipan until soft and then roll out into a circle and use to cover the base of the chilled flan. Cream the margarine and sugar until light and then stir in the grated apple. Whisk the egg whites until stiff and fold into the apple mixture. Spoon into the lined flan case. Arrange the pastry trimmings over the top of the flan to form a lattice and then brush with the remaining yolk to glaze. Bake in the oven for about 40 minutes until a light golden brown.

to freeze   Wrap well with foil, seal, label and freeze.

to thaw   Thaw at room temperature for about 6 hours before serving.

Simple Lemon Syllabub

A useful sweet to have in the freezer. Lemon cheese can be bought in most leading supermarkets.

serves 8

juice of 1 lemon
¼ pint (150ml) lemon cheese
¼ pint (150ml) sweet white wine
½ pint (300ml) double cream

Whisk all ingredients together in a bowl until thick and will stand in peaks. Spoon into 8 ramekin dishes.

to serve now   Chill before serving.

to freeze   Cover the tops firmly with foil and stack carefully in the freezer.

to thaw   Thaw overnight in the refrigerator before serving.

Raspberry Fool

A good way of using up the last pickings of home-grown raspberries that are a bit mushy.

serves 8
2 lb (900g) frozen raspberries, thawed
6 oz (175g) caster sugar
1 egg white
½ pint (300ml) whipping cream, whipped

Process raspberries in a processor or blender until smooth, and then sieve to remove the seeds. Stir sugar into purée. Whisk egg white in a bowl until stiff then fold gently into the purée with the cream until well blended. Pour into a 3 pint (1.75 litre) freezer-proof serving dish and refrigerate or freeze.

to freeze
Open freeze then wrap in a double thickness of foil, seal, label and return to the freezer.

to thaw
Thaw at room temperature for about 4 hours before serving.

Apple Mousse

A super light pudding which goes well after a heavy main course.

serves 6

2 lb (900g) cooking apples, peeled, cored and sliced
3 oz (75g) caster sugar
grated rind and juice of 1 lemon
3 eggs, separated
½ oz (15g) powdered gelatine
3 tablespoons cold water
¼ pint (150ml) whipping cream, whipped

Put the apples in a pan with a little water and simmer gently until tender. Allow to cool slightly then put them with sugar, lemon rind and juice and egg yolks in a processor or blender. Reduce to a purée.

Put the gelatine in a small bowl with the cold water, allow to stand for about 5 minutes to form a sponge, then heat over a pan of simmering water until the gelatine is dissolved and clear. Remove from the heat, allow to cool, then stir into the apple mixture.

Whisk the egg whites until stiff with an electric or rotary whisk then fold with the whipped cream into the apple mixture. Be sure to mix them well together. Pour the mousse into a 2 pint (1.2 litre) soufflé dish and chill in the fridge until set.

to freeze

Open freeze in dish then wrap in foil, seal, label and return to the freezer.

to thaw

Thaw in the refrigerator for about 8 hours.

Blackcurrant Mousse

This can be made at any time of year if you have blackcurrants in the freezer. It has a lovely sharp flavour.

serves 6

1 lb (450g) blackcurrants
6 oz (175g) caster sugar
3 eggs, separated
½ oz (15g) powdered gelatine
3 tablespoons water
juice of ½ lemon
¼ pint (150ml) whipping cream, whipped

Put the blackcurrants and sugar in a pan and simmer gently for about 15 minutes until soft then sieve. This gives about ½ pint (300ml) purée. Whisk ¼ pint (150ml) of this with the egg yolks until thick.

Put the gelatine in a small bowl with the water, leave to stand for about 5 minutes to form a sponge, then dissolve the gelatine over a pan of simmering water until clear. Remove from the heat and allow to cool. Stir into the blackcurrant and yolk mixture with the lemon juice. Whisk the egg whites with an electric or rotary whisk until stiff then carefully fold them into the blackcurrant, yolk and gelatine mixture with the cream.

Pour the mousse into a 2 pint (1.2 litre) soufflé dish and leave in the fridge to set.

If serving at once, pour the rest of the purée over the top of the mousse, when it's set.

to freeze

Pack purée in a small lidded plastic container and label. Wrap the mousse in cling film, label separately, then freeze both.

to thaw

Thaw mousse and purée in the refrigerator overnight or at room temperature for about 6 hours. Pour purée from container on top of mousse before serving.

Mocha Pots

A very rich pudding so serve after a fairly light meal.

serves 6

1 oz (25g) butter
6 oz (175g) plain chocolate, broken into squares
2 tablespoons rum
3 teaspoons instant coffee, dissolved in 1 tablespoon hot water
4 eggs, separated
¼ pint (150ml) whipping cream, whipped

Put the butter and chocolate in a bowl over a pan of simmering water and allow to melt. Add the rum and coffee. Stir in the egg yolks and mix well. Remove from the heat and allow to cool.

Whisk the egg whites with an electric or rotary whisk until they form peaks, gently fold in the chocolate mixture then pour into 6 ramekin dishes. Leave in the fridge to set then decorate with a swirl of whipped cream.

to freeze

Open freeze before decorating, wrap, seal and label then return to the freezer.

to thaw

Thaw in the refrigerator overnight and decorate with cream before serving.

Fresh Cream Chocolate Colettes

These must be served very cold otherwise they are too runny.

makes about 30

8 oz (225g) plain chocolate
about 30 petits fours cases

filling
10 tablespoons home-made lemon curd
¼ pint (150ml) double cream, whipped

Break the chocolate into pieces, put in a bowl and melt gently over a pan of simmering water. Remove bowl from the heat and use melted chocolate to line the insides of the paper cases. Spread the chocolate around the base and sides of each case using the handle of a teaspoon. Put the cases in the refrigerator to set and then repeat later with another layer of chocolate. Chill until set.

To prepare the filling, stir 7 tablespoons of the lemon curd into the whipped cream. Put into a piping bag fitted with a rose nozzle and pipe some filling into each chocolate case so that it comes almost to the top. Spoon a little of the remaining lemon curd on top of each. Chill well before serving.

to freeze   Open freeze then pack in one layer in a shallow rigid container, seal, label and return to the freezer.

to thaw   Thaw in the refrigerator for about 8 hours before serving.

Boozy Oranges

Serve really cold.

serves 4
8 thin skinned oranges
3 oz (75g) caster sugar

for serving only
4 tablespoons brandy

Finely grate the rind of 2 of the oranges. Using a sharp knife, cut the peel from all the oranges so that the pith is completely removed. Cut the oranges in thin slices, and put them in a rigid container. Sprinkle with the grated rind and sugar.

to freeze
Cover, label and freeze.

to thaw
Thaw overnight in the refrigerator, and stir in the brandy just before serving.

Special Fruit Salad

A good recipe to prepare if fruit is particularly reasonable in price.

serves 10-12

1 grapefruit, segmented
2 thin skinned oranges, segmented
1 pineapple, cut into chunks
1 honeydew melon, cut into cubes
8 oz (225g) black grapes, cut in half and seeded
8 oz (225g) eating apples, peeled, cored and sliced
4 oz (100g) caster sugar

Arrange the fruit and sugar in layers in a rigid container. Do not use over-ripe fruits as they will soften in the freezer.

to freeze Cover, label and freeze.

to thaw Thaw overnight in the refrigerator. If liked add more fruit, such as bananas, pears and cherries, and stir in 2 tablespoons orange liqueur.

HOT PUDDINGS

The freezer is useful for lengthy storage of things like breadcrumbs to use for treacle tart and fruit charlottes. Breadcrumbs are boring to make in small quantities but sensible to make a whole loaf at a time. Then just freeze in a polythene bag.

I keep shortcrust pastry in the freezer at the rubbed-in stage ready for pies. I find it hardly needs thawing before I use it. I simply add the usual amount of water. If I want to use it as a crumble I add some sugar—the family like demerara best.

Usually in my freezer I have a batch of 8 pancakes interleaved with greaseproof paper ready to thaw and use, perhaps filled with stewed apple, brown sugar and cinnamon or simply to fill with fresh raspberries and serve with icecream.

Raspberry and Apple Crumble

This is a pudding made entirely from items stored in your freezer. Freeze your own raspberries, stewed apple, and the crumble mix, then assemble when thawed for a delicious pudding.

serves 6
4 oz (100g) plain flour
2 oz (50g) ground almonds
3 oz (75g) margarine
2 oz (50g) light muscovado sugar
1 lb (450g) frozen sweetened stewed apple, thawed
12 oz (350g) frozen raspberries, thawed
1 oz (25g) flaked almonds

Heat the oven to 400°F/200°C/Gas 6.

To make the crumble, put the flour in a bowl with the almonds, and add the margarine cut in small pieces. Rub in with the finger tips until the mixture resembles fine breadcrumbs, then stir in the sugar.

Put both the thawed fruits in a pie dish and spoon over the crumble mixture and sprinkle with flaked almonds. Bake in the oven for about 40 minutes until the crumble and almonds are golden brown.

to freeze Freeze the fruits (see section at beginning of book) and crumble mixture separately, in rigid polythene containers.

to thaw Thaw at room temperature for about 3 hours then assemble and cook as above.

Apricot Upside Down Pudding

Delicious served warm with whipped cream.

serves 6-8

3 oz (75g) self-raising flour
3 oz (75g) soft margarine
3 oz (75g) caster sugar
1 egg, beaten
1 tablespoon apricot juice from can
½ level teaspoon baking powder

cake topping
8 oz (227g) can apricot halves, drained
2 glacé cherries, halved
2 oz (50g) light muscovado sugar

Put all the cake ingredients in a bowl and beat well for 2 minutes or until well blended.

Place the apricots, for the topping, cut side down with half a cherry in the middle, in the bottom of a well greased 7 inch (17.5cm) round shallow cake tin. Sprinkle over the sugar. Spread the cake mixture over the apricots and smooth the top.

to freeze   Freeze raw in the tin, wrapped in foil, sealed and labelled.

to thaw   Thaw at room temperature for about 6 hours. Heat the oven to 375°F/ 190°C/Gas 5 then bake the pudding for about 25 minutes or until the cake is well risen and golden brown. Leave to cool in the tin for about 20 minutes and then turn out on to a serving plate.

Apple Almond Pudding

A special family pudding for a chilly day.

serves 4-6
1 lb (450g) Bramley apples, peeled, cored and sliced
4 oz (100g) granulated sugar
4 oz (100g) soft margarine
4 oz (100g) caster sugar
2 eggs
2 oz (50g) ground almonds
2 oz (50g) semolina
1 oz (25g) flaked almonds

Cook apples gently in just a little water until tender, then remove from the heat and stir in the granulated sugar. Allow to cool.

Cream margarine and sugar until light and creamy, then beat in eggs a little at a time. Stir in ground almonds and semolina.

Spoon cooked apple into deep greased 7 inch (17.5cm) ovenproof dish then spread almond mixture on top and sprinkle with flaked almonds.

to serve now
Heat oven to 350°F/180°C/Gas 4. Bake for about 1 hour until golden brown.

to freeze
Freeze raw, wrapped in foil, sealed and labelled.

to thaw
Thaw at room temperature for about 6 hours then bake as above. Serve warm.

Syrup Fruit Pudding

Traditional, good, and so satisfying! Serve with lashings of custard.

serves 6-8
3 good tablespoons golden syrup, or more
4 oz (100g) shredded suet
4 oz (100g) currants
4 oz (100g) raisins, chopped
4 oz (100g) fresh white breadcrumbs
4 oz (100g) self-raising flour
1 teaspoon baking powder
about ½ pint (300ml) milk

Lightly butter a 2 pint (1.2 litre) pudding basin and put the golden syrup in the bottom. Stir together all the remaining ingredients until thoroughly mixed then spoon on top of the syrup. Cover the basin with a double layer of foil and steam over a pan of simmering water for about 2 hours until cooked through.

to freeze   Allow to cool, wrap with clean foil, seal, label and freeze.

to thaw   Thaw at room temperature for about 8 hours. Reheat over a pan of simmering water for about 30 minutes.

Baked Apple Ramekins

A very simple dish, which is handy to have individually in the freezer ready for cold days—they just need heating through.

serves 4

1 egg, beaten
4 oz (100g) golden granulated sugar
2 oz (50g) flour
1 teaspoon baking powder
1 large cooking apple, peeled, cored and chopped

Heat the oven to 350°F/180°C/Gas 4. Lightly butter 4 ramekin dishes.

Put all ingredients in a bowl and beat well for about 2 minutes until thoroughly mixed. Divide mixture between the prepared dishes.

to freeze Freeze before cooking, wrapped in foil, sealed and labelled.

to thaw Thaw at room temperature for about 4 hours then bake at 350°F/180°C/ Gas 4 for about 20 minutes until golden brown. Serve straight away, with whipped cream.

Old-Fashioned Fruit Compote

If there is some left serve chilled for breakfast.

serves 10

4 oz (100g) dried figs
4 oz (100g) dried apricots
4 oz (100g) dried peaches
4 oz (100g) dried prunes
4 oz (100g) dried apple rings
4 oz (100g) sultanas
1½ pints (900ml) water
8 oz (225g) light muscovado sugar
1 strip lemon rind
2 teaspoons ground nutmeg
2 teaspoons cinnamon

for serving only
a little brandy, if liked
at least ¼ pint (150ml) double cream, whipped

Put all fruits in a bowl with the water and leave to stand overnight.

Next day strain off water into a pan, add sugar, lemon rind and spices, and simmer gently for about 10 minutes. Add the fruit, cover with a lid, and continue to simmer for about an hour until the fruit is tender. Remove and discard the lemon rind and leave to cool.

to freeze   Freeze in a rigid container, cover and label.

to thaw   Thaw overnight in the fridge, reheat if liked, then add brandy if used, and serve with the whipped cream.

Mincemeat and Apple Pancakes

These take time to make, but they're lovely to serve and to eat.

serves 4-6

1 lb (450g) cooking apples, sliced
4 oz (100g) muscovado sugar
2 oz (50g) butter
½ teaspoon cinnamon
6 oz (175g) mixed dried fruit
1 tablespoon lemon juice
a little finely grated lemon rind

pancakes
4 oz (100g) plain flour
1 egg
1 tablespoon oil
½ pint (300ml) milk

for serving only
3 oz (75g) butter
¼ pint (150ml) double cream, whipped

Put the apples in a pan with the sugar, butter and cinnamon and simmer gently, stirring occasionally for about 20 minutes until tender. Stir in the dried fruit, lemon juice and rind and leave to cool.

To prepare the pancakes, sieve flour into a bowl. Blend in the egg with the oil and the milk. Heat a very little oil in an 8 inch (20cm) pan. Drop 2 tablespoons of the mixture into the pan and tilt and rotate to spread out the batter. Cook for 1 minute, then turn over and cook the other side for I minute. Turn out and make 7 more pancakes.

Divide the filling among the pancakes and roll up.

to freeze

Wrap each pancake in cling film and pack carefully in bags. Seal, label and freeze.

to thaw

Unwrap and thaw at room temperature for about 4 hours. Fry the pancake rolls in the butter until they are golden brown. Serve with plenty of whipped cream.

Raspberry and Almond Tart

Really almondy tasting, and it can be served either warm or cold.

serves 6
4 oz (100g) plain flour
1 oz (25g) butter
1 oz (25g) lard
about 1 tablespoon cold water

filling
4 oz (100g) butter
4 oz (100g) caster sugar
1 egg, beaten
4 oz (100g) ground rice
½ teaspoon almond essence
2 heaped tablespoons raspberry jam
2 oz (50g) flaked almonds

Heat the oven to 400°F/200°C/Gas 6.

Put the flour in a bowl and rub in fats until mixture resembles fine breadcrumbs. Add sufficient water to mix to a firm dough. Roll out thinly on a lightly floured surface and line an 8 inch (20cm) flan ring, which should be placed on a baking sheet. Prick the base with a fork and leave to rest in the refrigerator for about 5 minutes while making the filling.

Heat the butter in a pan until it has just melted then stir in the sugar and cook for a minute. Stir in the egg, ground rice and almond essence.

Spread the jam over the base of the pastry, pour the filling on top, and sprinkle with the almonds. Cook in the oven for about 30 minutes until risen and golden brown. Take out of oven, remove the flan ring and leave to cool.

to freeze
Open freeze, then wrap well in foil, label and return to freezer.

to thaw
Thaw at room temperature for about 6 hours before serving. Heat through in 325°F/160°C/Gas 3 oven for about 30 minutes if serving warm.

Treacle Tart

Always popular as a pudding. This recipe is for a family size tart, but for a party size tart, simply double all the ingredients and make in a 10½ inch (26cm) loose-bottomed fluted flan tin.

serves 6

4 oz (100g) plain flour
1 oz (25g) butter
1 oz (25g) lard
1 generous tablespoon cold water

filling
4 rounded tablespoons golden syrup
2 oz (50g) fresh white breadcrumbs
finely grated rind and juice of ½ lemon

First prepare the pastry. Put flour in a bowl and rub in fats to resemble fine breadcrumbs then mix to a firm dough with water. Knead gently until smooth then roll out on a lightly floured surface and use to line an 8 inch (20cm) loose-bottomed fluted flan tin. Chill flan case in the refrigerator. Heat the oven to 400°F/200°C/Gas 6, and place a heavy flat baking sheet on the centre oven shelf to heat through.

For the filling, warm the measured syrup in a pan until thin and runny. Stir in breadcrumbs and leave to stand for about 10 minutes until the crumbs have absorbed all the syrup. Stir in the lemon rind and juice. Take flan case out of fridge and spread filling in pastry case. Bake on the baking sheet in the oven for about 15 minutes then lower the heat to 350°F/180°C/Gas 4 and continue cooking for a further 20 minutes until set, and the edges of pastry are a pale golden brown. Serve either warm or cold.

to freeze

Allow to cool then open freeze. Wrap well in cling film, label and return to freezer.

to thaw

Thaw at room temperature for about 8 hours before serving. Heat through in 325°F/160°C/Gas 3 oven if serving warm.

Double Plate Mince Pie

Lots of filling and not too much pastry for a delicious pie that can be made and frozen up to 2 months before Christmas.

serves 6-8

2 oz (50g) butter
2 oz (50g) lard
6 oz (175g) plain flour
1 egg yolk
½oz (15g) caster sugar
about 2 teaspoons water
1 lb (450g) mincemeat
milk to glaze

Heat the oven to 400°F/200°C/Gas 6.

Rub fats into flour until the mixture resembles fine breadcrumbs. Mix the egg yolk, sugar and water together, add to the dry ingredients and bind them together. Divide the pastry in half, roll out one half and use to line an 8 inch (20cm) pie plate. Spread the mincemeat over the pastry.

Roll out remaining pastry, damp edges and use to cover the pie. Press firmly to seal the edges. Brush the pastry with a little milk and bake in the oven for about 25 minutes until pale golden brown.

to freeze Cool, then cover with a polythene bag, seal, label and freeze.

to thaw Thaw at room temperature for about 4 hours then reheat in the oven for about 20 minutes and serve warm with brandy or rum butter.

Devon Apple Pie

Traditional and good, this is a *really* handy pud to have in the freezer. You can always add other fruits to the pie, such as blackberries, raspberries or rhubarb.

serves 6-8

1 ½ lb (675g) cooking apples, sliced
4 oz (100g) muscovado sugar
2 oz (50g) butter
1 teaspoon ground cinnamon

pastry
8 oz (225g) flour
2 oz (50g) butter
2 oz (50g) lard
about 2 tablespoons cold water

for serving only
milk to glaze

Put the apples in a pan with the sugar, butter and cinnamon. Cook gently until the apples are just tender, stirring occasionally. Leave to cool.

To make up the pastry, rub the fat into the flour until it resembles fine breadcrumbs, and mix to a dough with water. Use half the pastry to line an 8 inch (20cm) pie plate. Spread in the filling. Moisten the edges with water and roll out the remaining pastry to cover. Press edges well together and flute, using any trimmings to decorate the pie.

Heat the oven to 425°F/220°C/Gas 7 and bake for about 35 minutes after glazing with milk.

to freeze Freeze without baking, wrapped in foil, labelled and sealed.

to thaw Remove wrapping, glaze with a little milk and bake straight from frozen as above, but allowing an extra 10 minutes.

Garden Fruit Pie

Lovely to freeze away in the summer and then eat during the winter.

serves 4-6
8oz (225g) blackberries
8oz (225g) raspberries
8oz (225g) blackcurrants
8oz (225g) rhubarb, cut into 1 inch (2.5cm) lengths
4oz (100g) caster sugar
2 tablespoons cold water

pastry
6oz (175g) plain flour
1 ½ oz (40g) margarine
1 ½ oz (40g) lard
about 6 teaspoons cold water

for serving only
milk to glaze
granulated sugar

Put a pie funnel in the centre of a 2 pint (1.2 litre) pie dish.

Mix all the fruits together; put half in the bottom of the pie dish and sprinkle with the sugar. Cover with the remaining fruit and water.

Make up the pastry in the usual way (see previous recipe), then roll out on a floured surface to cover the top of the pie dish, using any trimmings to decorate. Chill in the refrigerator for 30 minutes.

to serve now
Heat the oven to 400°F/200°C/Gas 6. Brush the pie with a little milk and sprinkle the top with granulated sugar. Make a small slit in the centre for the steam to escape. Bake in the oven for about 40 minutes until the fruit is tender and the pastry crisp and golden brown.

to freeze
Freeze without glazing and baking, wrapped in foil and labelled.

to thaw
Thaw at room temperature for about 6 hours and then bake as above. Serve hot with vanilla ice cream.

Cranberry and Apple Crunch

Not only do cranberries taste delicious with apples and orange juice, but the pastry, with its added sugar and walnuts, is really quite special. Serve with whipped cream.

serves 6

6 oz (175g) plain flour
1½ oz (40g) lard
1½ oz (40g) margarine
1 oz (25g) caster sugar
1 oz (25g) finely chopped walnuts
generous tablespoon water

topping
8 oz (225g) fresh cranberries
1½ lb (675g) cooking apples, peeled, cored and sliced
grated rind and juice of 1 orange
4 oz (100g) caster sugar

Heat the oven to 400°F/200°C/Gas 6, and put a baking tray in oven to heat through.

Put flour in a bowl and rub in fat until mixture resembles fine breadcrumbs. Stir in the sugar and chopped nuts, and bind dough together with water. Roll out on a lightly floured surface and use to line an 8 inch (20cm) loose-bottomed flan tin. Chill in the fridge for about 10 minutes then lift on to the baking tray, which will have warmed through, and bake blind with greaseproof paper and baking beans for about 20 minutes. Remove the paper and beans for the last 5 minutes.

Meanwhile simmer the cranberries, apples, orange rind and juice for about 10 minutes until beginning to soften, then remove from the heat and stir in the sugar.

to serve now

Pour the fruit mixture into the flan case and return to the oven for about another 20 minutes until the fruit is tender and the flan just beginning to colour.

to freeze

Pack the flan case and filling separately (the former wrapped in foil, the latter in a small polythene container), label and freeze.

to thaw

Thaw at room temperature for about 6 hours then assemble the flan and bake as above.

CAKES AND

BISCUITS

I really have found that fruit cakes improve and mature with freezing. I have a friend who makes wedding cakes as a small business and he likes to freeze them un-iced for at least 6 months. It is also extremely reassuring to know that you have a cake in the freezer for any unexpected weekend callers.

If you are freezing a decorated cake, open-freeze it, completely finished, until frozen solid, then wrap in clingfilm and slip into a polythene box if you have one the right size. If not, double wrap and put it in the part of the freezer where it won't get knocked.

Should you have a few slices of a special cake left and you don't want to eat it up, wrap the slices individually and freeze for another occasion. A very good solution for dieters who do not want to be tempted by the cake tin!

Apple Cake

This cake is delicious served warm with cream.

6 oz (175g) self-raising flour
1 level teaspoon baking powder
6 oz (175g) caster sugar
2 eggs
½ teaspoon almond essence
4 oz (100g) butter, melted
12 oz (350g) cooking apples, peeled, cored and sliced

for serving only
caster sugar
¼ pint (150ml) single cream

Heat the oven to 350°F/180°C/Gas 4 and line, with greased greaseproof paper, an 8 inch (20cm) loose-bottomed cake tin.

Put the flour and baking powder in a bowl with the sugar. Beat the eggs and essence together and stir them into the flour, together with the melted butter, and mix well. Spread half this mixture into the tin. Arrange the apples on the cake mixture. Spoon the remaining mixture in blobs over the top of the apples.

Bake in the oven for 1¼ hours until golden brown and shrinking away from the sides of the tin. Leave to cool for 15 minutes and then turn out and remove the paper.

to freeze Wrap well with cling film, label and freeze.

to thaw Thaw at room temperature for about 6 hours. Sift over the caster sugar and then serve warm, with cream.

RIGHT: *Apple Cake (above)*

Sunday Tea Chocolate Cake

This amount makes two cakes.

10 oz (275g) caster sugar
6 tablespoons water
3 oz (75g) cocoa
¼ pint (150ml) milk
8 oz (225g) soft margarine
4 eggs, separated
8 oz (225g) self-raising flour
2 level teaspoons baking powder
½ pint (300ml) whipping cream, whipped

icing
3 oz (75g) butter
2 oz (50g) cocoa, sieved
6 tablespoons milk
8 oz (225g) icing sugar, sieved

Heat the oven to 350°F/180°C/Gas 4. Grease and line with greased greaseproof paper 2 x 8 inch (20cm) sandwich tins.

Put 3 oz (75g) of the caster sugar in a pan with the water and cocoa and mix to a thick paste. Cook gently until the mixture is thick and shiny. Stir in the milk and leave to cool.

Cream the margarine with remaining sugar. Beat in the egg yolks with the cocoa mixture, then fold in the flour and baking powder. Whisk the egg whites until stiff then fold them into the mixture too. Divide between the tins and bake for about 40 minutes until the cakes spring back when lightly pressed with a finger. Turn them out, peel off paper and leave to cool on a wire rack.

To make the icing, melt the butter in a small pan, stir in the cocoa and cook gently for 1 minute. Remove from heat, and beat in milk and icing sugar. Leave to cool, stirring occasionally until icing has thickened. Split each cake in half, and sandwich cakes together with whipped cream. Spread chocolate icing over the tops.

to freeze   Wrap each cake with foil, label and freeze.

to thaw   Leave to thaw at room temperature for about 5 hours.

LEFT: *Sunday Tea Chocolate Cake (above)*

Good Family Chocolate Cake

Make in a foil container and then pour the icing on once it has cooled. There are no drips of icing to mop up or waste, as no cooling rack is used.

1 rounded tablespoon cocoa
2 tablespoons hot water
4 oz (100g) soft margarine
4 oz (100g) caster sugar
2 large eggs
4 oz (100g) self-raising flour
1 level teaspoon baking powder

icing
1½ oz (40g) hard margarine
1 oz (25g) cocoa, sieved
2 tablespoons milk
4 oz (100g) icing sugar, sieved

Heat the oven to 350°F/180°C/Gas 4, and grease and line an 8 inch (20cm) round foil cake tin with greased greaseproof paper. If using a foil container then grease well.

Blend the cocoa and water in a large bowl. Add the remaining cake ingredients to the bowl and beat well for about 2 minutes until well blended. Turn into the prepared tin and bake in the oven for about 35 minutes. When the cake is cooked it will have shrunk slightly from the sides of the tin and the cake will spring back when lightly pressed with a finger.

Now prepare the icing. Melt the margarine in a small pan, stir in the cocoa and cook gently for a minute. Remove from the heat and add the milk and icing sugar. Beat well to mix and then leave to cool, stirring occasionally until the icing has thickened to a spreading consistency. Spread over the top of the cake and leave to set.

to freeze   Open freeze then wrap well with foil, seal, label and return to freezer.

to thaw   Unwrap and leave to thaw at room temperature for about 8 hours before serving.

Chocolate and Lemon Cake

Rich and luxurious for a special occasion; for everyday, leave off the chocolate topping.

6 oz (175g) soft margarine
6 oz (175g) caster sugar
6 oz (175g) self-raising flour
1 level teaspoon baking powder
finely grated rind of 2 lemons
3 eggs
2 tablespoons milk

lemon syrup
juice of 2 lemons
4 oz (100g) caster sugar

chocolate topping, for serving only
2 oz (50g) hard margarine
2 level tablespoons cocoa
1 level tablespoon golden syrup

Heat the oven to 375°F/190°C/Gas 5. Line a 2 lb (900g) loaf tin with greased greaseproof paper.

Put all the cake ingredients in a large bowl and beat well for 2 minutes until they are all blended. Turn into the prepared tin and bake in the oven for about an hour until well risen and golden brown. A warm skewer should come out clean when pushed into the centre of the cake.

For the syrup, mix the lemon juice and caster sugar together then, while the cake is still warm, prod the top of the cake with a skewer and pour the lemon syrup over.

to serve now Allow the cake to cool then prepare the chocolate topping. Heat the margarine, cocoa and syrup in a pan, and stir until mixed. Allow to cool until it will coat the back of a spoon, then spread evenly over the top of the cake.

to freeze Freeze the cake without chocolate topping, wrapped in double thickness of foil and labelled.

to thaw Thaw at room temperature for about 6 hours then make chocolate topping to decorate cake as above.

Ginger and Chocolate Cake

To make the cake more special if you like, after thawing ice it with a thin glacé icing using the stem ginger syrup instead of water to mix.

4 oz (100g) self-raising flour
2 oz (50g) ground rice
6 oz (175g) butter, softened
6 oz (175g) light muscovado sugar
1 teaspoon ground ginger
1 level teaspoon baking powder
4 oz (100g) stem ginger, well drained and chopped
1 oz (25g) ground almonds
1 oz (25g) plain chocolate, grated
3 eggs

Heat the oven to 350°F/180°C/Gas 4. Grease and line with greased greaseproof paper a 7 inch (17.5cm) deep round cake tin.

Put all the ingredients in a large bowl and beat well for about 2 minutes until smooth, then turn the mixture into the prepared tin. Bake in the oven for about an hour until well risen, and a warm skewer comes out clean when pressed into the centre of the cake.

to freeze   Allow cake to cool then open freeze, wrap well in cling film or foil, seal, label and return to freezer.

to thaw   Thaw at room temperature for about 8 hours before serving.

Dundee Cake

A first-rate fruit cake. Be sure not to add too much marmalade otherwise it is very likely to sink.

6 oz (175g) soft margarine
3 oz (75g) caster sugar
3 oz (75g) dark muscovado sugar
12 oz (350g) mixed dried fruit
3 large eggs, beaten
9 oz (250g) self-raising flour
2 oz (50g) glacé cherries, quartered
2 level tablespoons marmalade
2 oz (50g) halved almonds

Heat the oven to 325°F/160°C/Gas 3. Grease and line with greased greaseproof paper an 8 inch (20cm) deep round cake tin.

Put all the ingredients except the almonds in a bowl and mix well until blended. Turn into the lined tin and spread evenly. Arrange the almonds over the top of the mixture. Bake just above the centre of the oven for about 2 hours; when the cake is pierced with a fine warm skewer in the centre it will come out clean if ready.

to freeze   Wrap when cold in a double thickness of foil, seal, label and freeze.

to thaw   Unwrap and thaw at room temperature for about 8 hours.

Tunis Cake

Over the years I have had many requests for a recipe for this cake—a sort of Madeira with a chocolate fudge icing.

8 oz (225g) self-raising flour
1 level teaspoon baking powder
6 oz (175g) caster sugar
6 oz (175g) softened butter
finely grated rind of 1 lemon
2 oz (50g) ground almonds
3 large eggs

chocolate topping
3 oz (75g) butter
2 oz (50g) cocoa, sieved
4 tablespoons milk
8 oz (225g) icing sugar, sieved

decoration
3 oz (75g) softened butter
6 oz (175g) icing sugar, sieved
a few drops of red and yellow food colouring

Heat the oven to 325°F/160°C/Gas 3 and line a deep 8 inch (20cm) cake tin with greased greaseproof paper.

Put all the cake ingredients in a large mixing bowl and beat well until smooth. Turn into the prepared tin, level the top and bake for about an hour until well risen and golden brown (and a warm skewer comes out clean when pushed into centre of cake). Allow to cool in the tin for 10 minutes, turn out on to wire rack, remove paper and leave until cold.

For chocolate topping, melt butter then stir in cocoa and cook for 2 minutes. Remove from heat, stir in milk and icing sugar, and mix until smooth. Cool until thick enough to coat the back of a spoon. Wrap a band of doubled foil around the cooled cake so that it comes ¾ inch (2cm) above the top and secure with freezer tape. Pour chocolate topping over cake and allow to set.

To make the decoration, beat butter and icing sugar together until smooth, divide in half, and colour one half red, the other yellow. Pipe alternate rings with a fine rose nozzle on top of cake, starting with a big circle round the outside and working in to the middle.

to freeze
Open freeze then wrap in foil, seal, label and return to freezer.

to thaw
Unwrap and allow to thaw at room temperature for about 8 hours.

Madeira Cake

To give a special look to the cake place a thin slice of citrus peel on the top of the cake half an hour after it has been in the oven. The butter should be soft and creamy not oily.

8 oz (225g) self-raising flour
1 level teaspoon baking powder
6 oz (175g) caster sugar
6 oz (175g) softened butter
finely grated rind of 1 lemon
2 oz (50g) ground almonds
3 large eggs

Heat the oven to 325°F/160°C/Gas 3 and line a deep 7 inch (17.5cm) cake tin with greased greaseproof paper.

Measure all the ingredients into a large bowl and beat well until smooth. Turn the mixture into the prepared tin, smooth the top, and bake in the oven for about 1¼ hours until well risen and golden brown. To test if the cake is done push a fine warm skewer into the centre of the cake; if it comes out clean the cake is done. Cool the cake in the tin for about 10 minutes then turn out, remove the paper, and continue to cool on a wire rack.

to freeze   Wrap in a double thickness of foil, seal, label and freeze.

to thaw   Unwrap and thaw at room temperature for about 5 hours.

Pineapple Fruit Cake

As this is a very moist cake, it is best kept in the refrigerator, and eaten within 6 weeks. I have known it to go mouldy if left in a cake tin in a warm kitchen.

2 oz (50g) glacé cherries, halved
7 oz (200g) self-raising flour
8 oz (225g) can pineapple pieces, drained
5 oz (150g) soft margarine
5 oz (150g) light muscovado sugar
2 eggs, beaten
2 tablespoons milk
12 oz (350g) mixed dried fruit

Heat the oven to 325°F/160°C/Gas 3. Grease and line with greased greaseproof paper an 8 inch (20cm) round cake tin. Roll the cherries in flour and finely chop the drained pineapple.

In a bowl cream the margarine and sugar, then gradually beat in the eggs. Gently fold in the flour, milk and fruit, including cherries and pineapple.

Turn into the prepared tin, smooth the top and bake in the oven for about 2 hours until the cake is a pale golden brown and shrinking from the sides of the tin. Leave in the tin until quite cold before turning out. Store in the refrigerator.

to freeze Wrap in a double thickness of foil, seal, label and freeze.

to thaw Thaw in the refrigerator overnight.

Cinnamon and Ginger Fruit Cake

A plain family fruit cake that improves with freezing. As it is low in fat, eat within a few days while it is moist. If liked, add grated orange rind to the cake too.

makes about 24 squares

8 oz (225g) self-raising flour
1 level teaspoon baking powder
3 level teaspoons ground ginger
1 level teaspoon ground cinnamon
4 oz (100g) soft margarine
4 oz (100g) light muscovado sugar
1 rounded tablespoon black treacle
1 rounded tablespoon golden syrup
2 oz (50g) glacé cherries, chopped
4 oz (100g) sultanas
2 eggs
5 tablespoons milk

icing
8 oz (225g) icing sugar
¼ teaspoon ground cinnamon
juice of ½ orange

Heat the oven to 350°F/180°C/Gas 4. Grease and line with greased greaseproof paper a 10 x 8 inch (25 x 20cm) roasting tin.

Put all ingredients for the cake in a large bowl and beat well for about 2 minutes until well blended. Turn mixture into prepared tin and bake for about an hour until well risen and a warm skewer comes out clean when pressed into the centre of the cake.

For the icing, mix icing sugar and cinnamon with orange juice to a spreading consistency. Spread over cake when it has cooled.

to freeze Open freeze in tin, then turn out and wrap well in cling film. Seal, label and return to the freezer.

to thaw Thaw at room temperature for about 8 hours. Serve cut into squares.

Easy Mincemeat Cake

I used to put a whole jar of mincemeat in this cake but I find it less crumbly and better with the smaller quantity.

5 oz (150g) soft margarine
5 oz (150g) light muscovado sugar
2 eggs
8 oz (225g) self-raising flour
4 oz (100g) currants
8 oz (225g) mincemeat
1 oz (25g) flaked almonds

Heat the oven to 325°F/160°C/Gas 3, and grease and line with greased greaseproof paper an 8 inch (20cm) round cake tin.

Place all the ingredients except the almonds in a large bowl and beat well for 1 minute or until well blended. Turn into the prepared tin, smooth the top and then sprinkle over the almonds.

Bake in the oven for about 1¾ hours until the cake is golden brown and shrinking away from the sides of the tin. Leave to cool in the tin, then take out and remove the paper.

to freeze   Wrap well with cling film, label and freeze.

to thaw   Thaw at room temperature for about 7 hours before serving.

American Walnut Slice

This recipe is a good way of using up egg whites. It is also rather on the sweet side, as it is American.

makes about 20 slices

1 oz (25g) cornflour
8 oz (225g) plain flour
3 level teaspoons baking powder
6 oz (175g) unsalted butter, softened
12 oz (350g) caster sugar
scant 8 fl. oz (225ml) milk
4 egg whites
3 oz (75g) chopped walnuts

topping
8 oz (225g) icing sugar, sieved
2 tablespoons water
2 oz (50g) chopped walnuts
2 oz (50g) glacé cherries, chopped

Heat the oven to 325°F/160°C/Gas 3. Grease and line with greased greaseproof paper a 7 x 11 inch (17.5 x 27.5cm) roasting tin.

Sift cornflour, flour and baking powder on to a plate. Cream the butter and sugar in a large bowl until light and fluffy, then stir in the flour and milk alternately until blended. Whisk the egg whites until stiff, fold into the cake mixture with the nuts, then turn into the tin. Bake in the oven for about 50 minutes until well risen. The top will be springy and the side of the cake shrinking away from the paper. Cool and remove the paper.

To make the topping, mix the icing sugar and water to a smooth icing and spread over the cake. Sprinkle the walnuts and cherries over the top.

to freeze Open freeze, then wrap in double thickness of foil, seal, label and return to freezer.

to thaw Unwrap and thaw at room temperature for about 8 hours before serving, divided into slices.

Coffee Walnut Cake

For a change leave the nuts out of the cake mixture and decorate with toasted flaked almonds.

4 oz (100g) soft margarine
4 oz (100g) caster sugar
4 large eggs
2 oz (50g) chopped walnuts
1 good tablespoon coffee essence
8 oz (225g) self-raising flour
1½ level teaspoons baking powder

coffee icing
3 oz (75g) soft margarine
8 oz (225g) icing sugar, sieved
1 tablespoon milk
1 tablespoon coffee essence

decoration
2 oz (50g) chopped walnuts

Heat the oven to 325°F/160°C/Gas 3. Grease and line with greased greaseproof paper 2 x 8 inch (20cm) sandwich tins.

Place the margarine, sugar, eggs, walnuts and coffee essence in a mixing bowl and then sieve in the flour and baking powder. Beat well until smooth and blended. Divide the mixture between the prepared tins and smooth the tops. Cook in the oven for about 35 minutes or until the cakes are well risen and spring back when pressed with your finger. Cool for 5 minutes and then turn out of the tins and remove the paper.

For the icing, place the margarine, icing sugar, milk and coffee essence in a bowl and beat until smooth. Use one-third to sandwich the cold cakes together and then spread the remainder over the cake and sprinkle with the chopped walnuts.

to freeze   Wrap in a double thickness of foil, seal, label and freeze.

to thaw   Unwrap and thaw at room temperature for about 6 hours.

Lemon Sponge Fingers

Popular with all ages, this light sponge mixture is deliciously lemony.

**makes
about 20
slices**

*4 oz (100g) soft margarine
1 level teaspoon baking powder
6 oz (175g) self-raising flour
6 oz (175g) caster sugar
2 eggs
4 tablespoons milk
finely grated rind of 1 lemon*

icing
*8 oz (225g) icing sugar, sieved
juice of 1 lemon*

Heat the oven to 350°F/180°C/Gas 4. Grease and line a 7 x 11 inch (27.5 x 17.5cm) roasting tin with greased greaseproof paper.

Put all the sponge ingredients in a large bowl and beat well for 2 minutes. Turn into the prepared tin and bake in the oven for about 50 minutes until the cake springs back when pressed with a finger and has shrunk from the sides of the tin.

Leave in the tin until quite cold then prepare the icing. Mix the sugar and lemon juice until smooth and spread evenly over the top of the cake.

to freeze   Open freeze *whole*, then wrap, seal and label. Return to the freezer.

to thaw   Thaw at room temperature then cut into fingers to serve.

Barabrith

A family standby and not too expensive to make. Start the day before.

5 oz (150g) currants
5 oz (150g) sultanas
5 oz (150g) light muscovado sugar
½ pint (300ml) hot tea
10 oz (275g) self-raising flour
1 egg

Put the fruit, sugar and tea in a bowl, cover and leave to stand overnight.

Heat the oven to 300°F/150°C/Gas 2. Grease and line with greased greaseproof paper an 8 inch (20cm) round cake tin.

Stir the flour and egg into the fruit mixture, and mix thoroughly. Turn into the lined tin and bake in the oven for about 1½ hours until cooked. Cool on a wire rack.

to freeze   Wrap in foil, seal, label and freeze.

to thaw   Thaw at room temperature for about 5 hours and serve sliced with butter.

Ovaltine Loaf

This is very easy to make and the children just love it. I usually make two loaves at a time, freeze one and eat the other straight away.

6 oz (150g) self-raising flour
2 tablespoons Ovaltine
1 oz (25g) light muscovado sugar
3 oz (75g) sultanas
2 tablespoons golden syrup
¼ pint (150ml) milk

Heat the oven to 350°F/180°C/Gas 4. Grease and line a 1 lb (450g) loaf tin with greased greaseproof paper.

Put all the ingredients together in a large bowl and mix well together until a thick batter is formed. Turn into the prepared tin and bake in the oven for about 60 minutes until the loaf is cooked. A fine warm skewer will come out clean when pushed into the centre of the cake. Turn out and leave to cool on a wire rack.

to freeze

Cool thoroughly, then wrap well in cling film, label and freeze.

to thaw

Thaw at room temperature for about 6 hours before serving in slices spread with butter.

Apricot and Cherry Fruitloaf

This is a very moist fruitloaf and should be kept in the fridge wrapped in foil rather than in a cake tin.

7 oz (200g) self-raising flour
4 oz (100g) glacé cherries, halved
15 oz (425g) can apricots
5 oz (150g) butter, softened
4½ oz (115g) light muscovado sugar
2 eggs, beaten
2 tablespoons milk
12 oz (350g) mixed dried fruit

Heat oven to 325°F/160°C/Gas 3. Grease and line with greased greaseproof paper a 2 lb (900g) loaf tin.

Put flour on a plate and roll three-quarters of the cherries in it, keeping the remainder for decoration. Drain apricots well and chop finely.

Cream the butter and sugar until light and soft. Beat in the eggs, adding a tablespoon of flour with the last amount of egg. Fold in the remaining flour, milk and all the fruit (except the cherries for decoration). Turn into the prepared tin and arrange the cherries on top. Bake in the oven for about 2 hours until pale golden brown or when a fine warm skewer pushed into the centre comes out clean. If some of the mixture still clings to the skewer give it a little longer. Turn out, remove paper and cool.

to freeze Wrap in a double thickness of foil, seal, label and freeze.

to thaw Unwrap and thaw at room temperature for about 8 hours before serving in slices.

Figgy Loaf

This has a rather different flavour but is quite delicious.

7 fl. oz (200ml) boiling water
6 oz (175g) dried figs, chopped
¾ level teaspoon bicarbonate of soda
6 oz (175g) light muscovado sugar
2 oz (50g) soft margarine
1 egg, beaten
8 oz (225g) self-raising flour
2 oz (50g) walnuts, chopped

Heat the oven to 350°F/180°C/Gas 4, and grease and line a 2 lb (900g) loaf tin with greased greaseproof paper.

Put the water, figs and bicarbonate of soda in a bowl and leave to stand for 5 minutes. Cream the sugar and margarine together until light and creamy then beat in the egg, together with the water and the figs. Add the flour and fold it into the mixture together with the walnuts.

Turn the mixture into the prepared tin, smooth the top, then bake in the oven for about an hour until cooked. Turn out, remove the paper and leave to cool on a wire rack.

to freeze   Wrap well with cling film, label and freeze.

to thaw   Thaw at room temperature for about 6 hours before serving.

Banana Loaf

A marvellous way of using over-ripe bananas.

4 oz (100g) soft margarine
6 oz (175g) caster sugar
2 eggs, beaten
2 ripe bananas, mashed
8 oz (225g) self-raising flour
1 teaspoon baking powder
2 tablespoons milk

Heat the oven to 350°F/180°C/Gas 4, and grease and line a 2 lb (900g) loaf tin with greased greaseproof paper.

Cream the margarine and sugar until light and soft then beat in the eggs and mashed bananas. Sift the flour and baking powder together then fold with the milk into the creamed mixture.

Pour into the prepared tin and bake in the centre of the oven for about an hour or until well risen and golden brown. Turn out and leave to cool on a wire rack with the paper removed.

to freeze   Wrap in a double thickness of foil, seal, label and freeze.

to thaw   Unwrap and thaw at room temperature for about 6 hours. Serve as it is or in slices spread with a little butter.

Granary Sultana Scones

For light scones the dough must be a bit sticky, a dry dough makes solid scones!

makes 10
4 oz (100g) wholemeal self-raising flour
4 oz (100g) white self-raising flour
2 level teaspoons baking powder
2 oz (50g) butter, softened
1 oz (25g) light muscovado sugar
2 oz (50g) sultanas
1 egg, beaten, made up to ¼ pint (150ml) with milk, plus about a further 2 tablespoons milk

Heat the oven to 425°F/220°C/Gas 7, and lightly grease a baking sheet.

Put the flours in a bowl with the baking powder and rub in the butter until the mixture resembles fine breadcrumbs. Stir in sugar and sultanas. Stir egg and milk into the flour and mix to a soft dough. Turn on to a lightly floured table, knead gently just to mix and pat out to ½ inch (1.5cm) thick. Cut into rounds with a 2½ inch (6cm) fluted cutter to make about 10 scones.

Place on the baking tray, brush the tops with a little milk and bake for about 10 minutes until pale golden brown. Remove from the baking tray and leave to cool on a cooling tray.

to freeze   Open freeze, then pack in bags, seal, label and return to freezer.

to thaw   Thaw at room temperature for about 6 hours.

Scotch Pancakes

Oddly enough these are called crumpets in many parts of Scotland!
Serve them warm with golden syrup.

**makes
about 18**

*sunflower oil for greasing
4 oz (100g) self-raising flour
1 teaspoon baking powder
1 oz (25g) caster sugar
1 egg
¼ pint (150ml) milk*

Prepare a heavy frying pan (or griddle) by rubbing salt on the surface
with a pad of kitchen paper and then greasing lightly with oil. When
ready to cook the pancakes, heat the frying pan until the oil is just hazy,
then wipe off any fat with kitchen paper.

Put the flour, baking powder and sugar in a bowl, add the egg and half
the milk and beat until smooth, then beat in the remaining milk. Spoon
the mixture on to the heated pan in rounds, spacing well. When bubbles
rise to the surface, turn the pancakes with a palette knife, and cook for
a further minute until golden brown.

to freeze

When cold, open freeze then stack together, separated by foil or
greaseproof paper, wrap in foil, seal, label, and return to the freezer.

to thaw

Spread on a tray, put in a cold oven and turn the heat to 400°F/200°C/
Gas 6 for about 15 minutes until warmed through.

Shortbread

It is essential for the shortbread to be pale brown underneath. If in doubt, just scoop out a little from the side of the tin to check the underneath.

makes 12 fingers

4 oz (100g) *plain flour*
2 oz (50g) *cornflour*
4 oz (100g) *butter*
2 oz (50g) *caster sugar*
icing sugar

Heat the oven to 325°F/160°C/Gas 3. Grease a 7 inch (17.5cm) square tin.

Sift the flour and cornflour together. Cream the butter and sugar together until light and soft then work in the flours and knead well together.

Press the mixture into the prepared tin and bake in the oven for about 35 minutes or until a very pale golden brown. Remove from the oven and mark into 12 fingers. Leave to cool in the tin.

to freeze

Freeze in the tin, turn out, and pack fingers in a polythene bag, return to freezer.

to thaw

Thaw at room temperature for about 6 hours. Dredge with sieved icing sugar and serve.

Lemon Freezer Biscuits

If liked, freeze in sausage shapes *before* baking, then thaw for about 30 minutes before cutting off slices and baking as below.

makes 32 biscuits

6 oz (175g) unsalted butter
finely grated rind of 1 lemon
4 oz (100g) caster sugar
8 oz (225g) plain flour
1 oz (25g) demerara sugar

Heat the oven to 325°F/160°C/Gas 3 and grease 2 or 3 large baking trays.

Cream the butter and lemon rind in a bowl until soft then beat in the sugar until the mixture is light. Blend in the flour and knead lightly until smooth. Divide the mixture in half, roll out to form two 6 inch (15cm) sausages, and cover these in demerara sugar. Wrap in foil and chill in the refrigerator until firm.

Cut each sausage into 16 slices and place on the baking sheets, allowing a little room for them to spread. Bake in the oven for about 25 minutes or until they are pale golden brown at the edges. Carefully lift off and leave to cool on a wire rack.

to freeze Pack carefully in polythene bags, seal, label and freeze.

to thaw Thaw at room temperature for about 4 hours.

Muesli Biscuits

Very crunchy and brittle but good for the health—and to taste!

makes about 20 biscuits

4 oz (100g) block margarine
3 oz (75g) granulated sugar
1 level tablespoon golden syrup
4 oz (100g) self-raising flour
4 oz (100g) breakfast muesli
1 level teaspoon bicarbonate of soda

Heat the oven to 350°F/180°C/Gas 4. Grease well one or two large baking trays.

Put the margarine, sugar and syrup in a pan and heat gently until the sugar has dissolved. Put the remaining ingredients in a bowl, pour in the melted mixture and mix well.

Spoon teaspoonfuls of the mixture on to the tray or trays, leaving room for them to spread. Bake in the oven for 12-15 minutes until golden brown. Leave to cool slightly before lifting them from the tray.

to freeze Pack in a rigid container, seal, label and freeze.

to thaw Thaw at room temperature for about 4 hours before serving.

Farmhouse Ginger Snaps

Rather than making a sausage with the mixture, it can be rolled into small balls and then baked. The children enjoy helping with this!

makes 50 biscuits

12 oz (350g) self-raising flour
4 oz (100g) demerara sugar
4 oz (100g) soft brown sugar
1 teaspoon bicarbonate of soda
3 teaspoons ground ginger
1 egg, beaten
4 oz (100g) butter
1 good tablespoon golden syrup

Mix all the dry ingredients together in a bowl then add the beaten egg, and the butter and golden syrup which have been melted together. Mix thoroughly. Divide the mixture in half and roll each into a long sausage 2 inches (5cm) in diameter. Wrap in cling film then chill in the refrigerator until firm (about an hour). Heat the oven to 325°F/160°C/ Gas 3.

Slice each sausage into 25 biscuits and place on greased baking trays. Pattern the top of the biscuits with a fork and bake in the oven for about 20 minutes until light golden brown. Lift off the baking trays and cool on a wire rack.

to freeze   Pack in a rigid container, cover, label and freeze.

to thaw   Remove from the container, and thaw at room temperature for about 2 hours.

Index